*Feminist Revision and the Bible*

THE BUCKNELL LECTURES IN LITERARY THEORY
*General Editors: Michael Payne and Harold Schweizer*

The lectures in this series explore some of the fundamental changes in literary studies that have occurred during the past thirty years in response to new work in feminism, Marxism, psychoanalysis, and deconstruction. They assess the impact of these changes and examine specific texts in the light of this new work. Each volume in the series includes a critical assessment of the lecturer's own publications, an interview, and a comprehensive bibliography.

# Feminist Revision and the Bible

## Alicia Suskin Ostriker

BLACKWELL
Oxford UK & Cambridge USA

First published 1993

Blackwell Publishers
238 Main Street, Suite 501
Cambridge, Massachusetts 02142
USA

108 Cowley Road
Oxford OX4 1JF
UK

*Library of Congress Cataloging-in-Publication Data*

A CIP catalog record for this book is available from the Library
of Congress

ISBN 0–631–18797–9 — 0–631–18798–7 (pbk.)

*British Library Cataloguing in Publication Data*

A CIP catalogue record for this book is available from the British
Library.

Typeset in 11 on 13 pt Plantin
by Pure Tech Corporation, Pondicherry, India
Printed in Great Britain by Biddles Ltd, Guildford
This book is printed on acid-free paper

# Contents

# Preface

Fundamental and far-reaching changes in literary studies, often compared to paradigmatic shifts in the sciences, have been taking place during the last thirty years. These changes have included enlarging the literary canon not only to include novels, poems, and plays by writers whose race, gender, or nationality had marginalized their work but also to include texts by philosophers, psychoanalysts, historians, anthropologists, social and religious thinkers, who previously were studied by critics merely as 'background'. The stance of the critic and student of literature is also now more in question than ever before. In 1951 it was possible for Cleanth Brooks to declare with confidence that the critic's job was to describe and evaluate literary objects, implying the relevance for criticism of the model of scientific objectivity while leaving unasked questions concerning significant issues in scientific theory, such as complementarity, indeterminacy, and the use of metaphor. Now the possibility of value-free skepticism is itself in doubt as many feminist, Marxist, and psychoanalytic theorists have stressed the inescapability of ideology and the consequent obligation of teachers and students of literature to declare their political, axiological, and aesthetic positions in order to make those positions conscious and available for examination. Such expansion and deepening of literary studies has, for many critics, revitalized their field.

Those for whom the theoretical revolution has been regenerative would readily echo, and apply to criticism, Lacan's call to revitalize psychoanalysis: 'I consider it to be an urgent task to disengage from concepts that are being deadened by routine use the meaning that they regain both from a re-examination of their history and from a reflexion on their subjective foundations. That, no doubt, is the teacher's prime function.'

Many practising writers and teachers of literature, however, see recent developments in literary theory as dangerous and anti-humanistic. They would insist that displacement of the centrality of the word, claims for the 'death of the author', emphasis upon gaps and incapacities in language, and indiscriminate opening of the canon threaten to marginalize literature itself. In this view the advance of theory is possible only because of literature's retreat in the face of aggressive moves by Marxism, feminism, deconstruction, and psychoanalysis. Furthermore, at a time of militant conservativism and the dominance of corporate values in America and Europe, literary theory threatens to diminish further the declining audience for literature and criticism. Theoretical books are difficult to read; they usually assume that their readers possess knowledge that few have who have received a traditional literary education; they often require massive reassessments of language, meaning, and the world; they seem to draw their life from suspect branches of other disciplines: professional philosophers usually avoid Derrida; psychoanalysts dismiss Freud as unscientific; Lacan was excommunicated even by the International Psycho-Analytical Association.

The volumes in this series record part of the attempt at Bucknell University to sustain conversation about changes in literary studies, the impact of those changes on literary art, and the significance of literary theory for the humanities and human sciences. A generous grant from the Andrew W. Mellon Foundation has made possible a five-year series of visiting lectureships by internationally known participants in the reshaping of literary studies. Each volume includes a comprehensive introduction to the published work of the lecturer, the two Bucknell Lectures, an interview, and a comprehensive bibliography.

## Acknowledgements

Grateful acknowledgement is made for permission to reprint from the following previously published material: 'if i stand in my window', 'good friday', and 'to a dark moses' copyright © 1987 by Lucille Clifton. Reprinted from *good woman: poems and a memoir 1969–1980* by Lucille Clifton with the permission of BOA Editions, Ltd, 92 Park Avenue, Brockport, NY, 14420; from 'the making of poems' and 'holy night' in *two-headed woman* by Lucille Clifton, copyright © 1980 by Lucille Clifton, reprinted by permission of Curtis Brown, Ltd., from *The Complete Poems of Emily Dickinson* edited by Thomas H. Johnson. Copyright 1929 by Martha Dickinson Bianchi; Copyright © renewed 1957 by Mary L. Hampson. Reprinted by permission of Little, Brown and Company; Dickinson poems also reprinted by permission of the publishers and the Trustees of Amherst College from *The Poems of Emily Dickinson*, Thomas H. Johnson, ed., Cambridge, Mass.: The Belknap Press of Harvard University Press, Copyright © 1951, 1955, 1983 by the President and Fellows of Harvard College; from *H. D. Collected Poems: 1912–1944*, copyright © 1982 by the Estate of Hilda Doolittle. Reprinted by permission of New Directions Publishing Corp. and Carcanet Press. 'Goblin Market' from *The Poetical*

*Works of Christina G. Rossetti* (New York: Macmillan, 1924), and 'Adam's Curse' from *The Poems of W. B. Yeats: A New Edition*, edited by Richard J. Finneran (New York: Macmillan, 1983). 'Myth' by Muriel Rukeyser from *Out of Silence*, 1992, Tri-Quarterly Books, Evanston IL © William L. Rukeyser.

# Introduction

Alicia Ostriker, like many contemporary American feminists, began her critical work with formal studies of male writers. Starting with *Vision and Verse in William Blake* (1965), a book-length examination of Blake's metrical techniques, she went on to write several articles on prosody in other male poets – Herbert, Tennyson, Wyatt and Surrey. The rebellious Blake, with what she terms his 'systematic detestation of the works and ways of patriarchal culture', provided an auspicious beginning (RE, p. 73). Many of the qualities that Ostriker finds later in women's poetry she found first in Blake – revisionary mythmaking, the embracing of contraries, the effort to transform human life, 'the interpenetration of the personal and the political', and the 'use of humor as a weapon against the sanctimonious' (RE, pp. 71, 83). In analyzing Blake's prosody, a thorny subject avoided by most Blake scholars, Ostriker connects Blake's prosodic choices to his politics, portraying his development as a search for 'liberated modes of verse' (VV, p. 6).

The interests of her early period continue into the present. Her more recent work on Blake includes the major project of editing the Penguin edition of *William Blake: The Complete Poems* (1977) as well as an influential essay on Blake and sexuality. She has also maintained her interest in technical questions, most likely because she is a working poet – one in a procession of feminist poet-critics such as Audre Lorde, Adrienne Rich, Alice Walker, Sandra Gilbert, and Rachel Blau DuPlessis. In fact, her needs as a woman artist first drew her to the poetry of other women whose work inspired her to make the traditional shift into a feminist critic's second stage, working on the art of women.

The first series of Alicia Ostriker's essays on American women poets was collected in *Writing Like a Woman* (1983). Besides discussions of H. D., Sylvia Plath, Anne Sexton, May Swenson, and Adrienne Rich, the volume contains two theoretical/personal essays on women and writing. Although she treats each of these poets separately, she already considers them part of a new literary movement, a renaissance of women that she chronicles in her next volume, *Stealing the Language: The Emergence of Women's Poetry in America* (1986).

These studies place her solidly in a major school of American feminist criticism – 'gynocritics' – named by Elaine Showalter, whose 1984–5 definition calls it a historically oriented criticism that 'looks at women's writing as it has actually occurred and tries to define its specific characteristics of language, genre, and literary influence, within a cultural network that includes variables of race, class, and nationality'.[1] According to Josephine Donovan, gynocritics is rooted in cultural feminism, a consideration of women's customs, epistemology, aesthetics and ethics.[2] Gynocritics has helped reintroduce history and politics into criticism. The material fact that many American feminist literary critics, Ostriker included, teach English in universities has rooted gynocritics in their political practice of reforming the university curriculum and in their work of teaching the predominantly female students in English studies.

Ostriker's gynocritical project is American women's poetry since 1960, a body of work she sees as 'a collec-

tive endeavor to redefine "woman" and "woman poet" '
(*SL*, p. 240). Believing that the core of a woman's art
movement is a concern with what it means to be a
woman, she writes mostly about poets who deal courage-
ously with the political 'realities' of women's lives.
Working to illuminate the place of women writers involves Ostriker, as it does most feminists, in what she
calls in the present volume a 'hermeneutic of desire'.
'First I see what I love', she explains, 'then I try to
understand it. . . . I like the word "love" better than the
word "evaluate" ' (DDP, p. 584). From those whose
affection for the word 'evaluate' exceeds Ostriker's, of
course, such a method provokes calls for more 'rigor'.[3]

Her critical strategy is to examine American women
poets in both traditional and radical terms. Such an
approach arises quite naturally from the American feminist literary critic's role as an insider/outsider whose
training in schools of criticism previous to feminism,
Jane Gallop points out, produces double loyalties – to
feminism and to literary criticism, to politics and to
literature, to practice and to theory, to women and to men,
to social considerations and to formalism.[4]

Accordingly, many of the qualities Ostriker discovers
in women poets are familiar from androcentric criticism
– innovation, philosophy, largeness, revisionary mythmaking, engagement with modern problems of alien-
ation, the invention of poetic forms to convey new
insights. Demanding for these poets a place in the traditional male literary history by claiming that they form a
coherent literary movement, she explicitly legitimates
their 'polemical' and 'necessarily adversarial' stance by
a comparison with romanticism and modernism, literary
movements which also had their polemical centers (*SL*,
pp. 7, 239). She further justifies the feminist politics of
contemporary women poets with a venerable romantic
claim, reminding us, in 'Dancing at the Devil's Party:
Some Notes on Politics and Poetry', of the Blakean

dictum that 'the true poet (the good poet) is necessarily the partisan of energy, rebellion, and desire, and is opposed to passivity, obedience, and the authority of reason, laws, and institutions' (DDP, p. 580). Of course, the application of such standard claims to the art of women is the reverse of orthodox.

Simultaneously, Ostriker finds in women's poetry motifs that have been redefined and revalued by feminism – the divided self, the body, anger, desire, and social concern. Pursuing the central gynocritical assumption that women's lives are sources of knowledge, she sees these motifs as grounded not in male tradition but in female experience.

Several of her views on women's poetry involve her in current critical controversies. Her conception of women's revisionary mythmaking embroils her in the current question of women's relationship to language. Like myth critics before her, Ostriker sees myths as 'the sanctuaries of language where our meanings for "male" and "female" are stored'. Therefore, revisionist mythmaking is the 'major strategy' whereby women writers 'subvert and overcome' the ' "oppressor's language" which denies them access to authoritative expression' (SL, p. 11). Rejecting a model of language as monolithically resistant to female expression, Ostriker asserts that 'semantically significant language is . . . only relatively and with many loopholes, masculine' (CCK, p. 133). Or else, she asks, 'How is it that women writers in our time have produced – in fiction, poetry, and drama, in and through a symbolic system that supposedly excludes the female and a set of genres that are supposedly dominated by masculinity – a substantial body of subversive and transformative work which redefines what we must mean by the terms *woman* and *literature*?' (CCK, p. 132).

Further critical debates rage around the issue of women's experience. Ostriker's vision of women poets writing from the lived experience of the material body could be read as perilously close to assigning women their old place in the body/mind dichotomy of patriarchal thought, but, for Ostriker, women's poetry heals this division: women 'represent the body as at one with the mind, an intelligently creative force' (*SL*, p. 197) – 'the gynocentric vision is not that the Logos condescends to incarnate itself, but that Flesh becomes Word' (*SL*, p. 199).

The gynocritical emphasis on experience entails a controversial interest in the lives of women poets. 'Books', says Nina Auerbach, 'are inseparable from the private experiences that authorized them'.[5] In *Writing Like A Woman* especially, Ostriker emphasizes biography, demonstrating how a woman poet's experience of leading a gender-defined life gives rise to the insights that inform her poetry. For Ostriker and other American feminists, the author is anything but dead.

American feminist insistence on the woman author and on women's experience has been attacked as naive empiricism, bourgeois individualism, and essentialism, but it does assert two major political points: that lived relations of domination give rise to political insights and that a revolution, in criticism and elsewhere, has to resist the oppression of a subject, an at-least-temporarily stable historical entity. The founding assumption of contemporary American feminist theory and practice is that the personal is the political. Donna Haraway states the central difficulty for feminists of dissolving the self: 'What kind of politics could embrace partial, contradictory, permanently unclosed constructions of personal and collective selves and still be faithful, effective – and, ironically, socialist feminist?'[6] In Ostriker's case, although she sees the woman poet as expressing 'self', this self is anything but classically unitary or romantically divided into a 'true' and 'false' self. She is at pains to demonstrate in *Stealing the Language* that women poets write of multiple selves constructed in response to their experiences, selves which 'challenge the validity of the I' (*SL*, p. 237).

A corollary of Ostriker's trust in experience is her distrust of literary theory – seemingly a strange position for a theorist, but one shared with many American feminists who suspect that much literary theory functions to maintain the interpretive hegemony of a male elite and may even be, in Elaine Showalter's words, a 'defensive reaction against the feminization of the profession'.[7] Nina Baym states this point of view succinctly: 'Not truth, but power, is the issue.'[8] American feminists often question the politics of theories not derived from the women's movement, especially theories that ignore gender or, in the case of some psychoanalytic theories, appear to reduce women to the non-verbal. As Ostriker ironically puts it, 'were I a good postmodernist I might learn from the master theoreticians of our time, or from their female disciples, that "woman" theoretically does not exist, that "she" is necessarily absence, lack' (RE, p. 67).

Ostriker claims that 'our critical discourse grows ever less capable of dealing with visionary artists as it grows ever more infatuated with pseudo-scientific postures and jargons' (RE, p. 84). In her view, theory often distorts reading because it is too narrowly interested in its own notions and in its own power over the reading situation. Out of respect for women, their poetry, and the experience from which it arises, she prefers 'to read by the light that poems themselves emit, rather than by the fixed beam of one or another theory which might shine where a poem is not and leave in darkness the place where it is' (*SL*, p. 13). Yet, while Ostriker deplores theory's interference in her 'personal responses', she clearly does not believe that reading is an innocent transaction: she realizes that personal responses have 'a political dimension', that 'we love what is on our side', and that there are no 'literary standards without ideological implications' (DDP, pp. 583–4). Thus, insisting that schemata-free reading is impossible, she seems simply to be cautioning against what she feels to be the current Urizenic focus on critical method at the expense of the reader, the poet, and the poem.

Distrust of theory is closely related to Ostriker's cultivation of a metaphoric and readable prose style. ' "No ideas but in metaphors" might be a useful rule of thumb for poets and critics', she suggests, 'especially when we engage in ideological discourse, where words so easily collapse into formulaic wallpaper. A metaphor gives us at least a fighting chance of saying something real' (DDP, p. 580). Accordingly, her critical prose is illuminated by eloquent figures such as 'the fiery muck of our bodies like oil spills burning' (WW, p. 146). Such a style, at once vivid and lucid, helps to make her prose accessible, a trait many American feminists value because of the duty they feel to return their work to a wide audience of women. As Patricia Hill Collins explains, 'I could not write a book about Black women's ideas that the vast majority of African-American women could not read and understand.'[9]

Ostriker's preference for the experiential and metaphoric over the abstract, and for revisionary mythmaking over against androcentric tradition, brings her to her third stage as a feminist critic – writing about Judaism and culture – a stage that reflects recent feminist critical interest in exploring difference especially through one's personal heritage. Her major work in progress during this period has been a series of critical rewritings of biblical narratives, at once mythical revision and cultural analysis, entitled *The Nakedness of the Fathers*.[10] Rethinking what she refers to as 'the founding text of western patriarchy' (NF, Preface), she has become 'one of those women who locate themselves deliberately at the intersection of literature, religion, and politics, and see their work as part of an effort to transform all three' (DDP, p. 594, n. 23). A Blakean embracing of contraries, *The Nakedness of the Fathers* exemplifies what Rachel Blau DuPlessis calls 'both/and vision', a trait of the revolutionary female aesthetic, 'born of shifts, contraries, negations, contradictions; linked to personal vulnerability and need', a vision that refuses to dichotomize and to choose one over another.[11] As Ostriker's Queen of Sheba states, 'The fool proposes either/or; the wise respond both/and' (WS, p. 152).

Ostriker's Jewish heritage, having endowed her with a thirst for knowledge and justice while denying her a place in its scholarly tradition, prompts both positive and negative reading strategies, the hermeneutics of suspicion and desire, the dual hermeneutic that Patrocinio Schweickart recommends for certain male texts that 'merit' it: 'a negative hermeneutic that discloses their complicity with patriarchal ideology, and a positive hermeneutic that recuperates the utopian moment – the authentic kernel – from which they draw a significant portion of their emotional power'.[12] These utopian moments recall the 'truths of Desire' that Ostriker considers the mark of true poetry (DDP, p. 580). It is these truths of Desire she wishes to recuperate from the Bible.

As part of the 'both/and' strategy, *The Nakedness of the Fathers* retells the stories of both male and female biblical figures. 'I *am* my fathers as much as I *am* my mothers' (NF, Preface), Ostriker asserts, aiming to include everyone, like Alice Walker's 'womanist' who is 'committed to the survival and wholeness of entire people, male and female'.[13] Reaching back in her desire to the patriarchs – herdsmen and family men, not warriors – Ostriker pictures herself longingly diving for them where they 'are alive in dream time' (NF, 'The Interpretation of Dreams'). In line with Nina Auerbach's advice to 'engorge' the patriarchy rather than isolate women in a ghetto of innocent victimization, she insists that women

'have to enter the tents/texts, invade the sanctuary, un-
cover the father's nakedness. We have to do it, believe
it or not, because we love him' (ET, p. 542).[14]

Her revision of the Bible is a veritable carnival of
both/and. Combining reading like a woman and writing
like a woman, she reads the Bible by rewriting it, em-
ploying what Adrienne Rich calls 're-vision'.[15] For
Ostriker, writing is reading, narrative discovers truth:
she asks, 'What do the stories mean to me and what do
I mean to them? I cannot tell until I write. . . . And then
each story opens like a flower, and I climb down into its
throat' (ET, p. 543). Emphasis on the reader rather than
the author as creator is an important departure from her
earlier work. In fact, as Ostriker points out, the Bible
was compiled by readers: 'acts of interpretation and reinterpretation form a large part of the canonized text
itself' (NF, Preface). With no poets in evidence to require her loyalty and care, she can read perhaps against
the grain, although still reading not by 'theory' but by
narrative and metaphor.

In The Nakedness of the Fathers, she blends a gynocritical recovery of the lost women of the Bible with a
critique of patriarchal texts and the creation of a new
women's literature. And she unites criticism and practice by not only critiquing but also overtly and deliberately transforming the text. Combining fiction, poetry,
and theory, she brings her careers as a creative writer
and as a critic/theorist together through her belief in
metaphor as a superior vehicle for ideas and her belief
in narrative for discovering meanings. So she rewrites
the stories – lyrically, beautifully, ironically, humorous-
ly, brutally – and provides footnotes from biblical scholarship, an explanatory introduction, and interspersed
passages of analysis, matching the Bible's multiplicity
with a protean creativity of her own. Into this Menip-
pean form she audaciously flings poetry, Black freedom songs, intensely poetic prose, Yiddish-influenced

American English (verging on stand-up comic in one case) – many voices. Even the ram sacrificed as a substitute for Isaac has a soliloquy. Using as many types and powers of language as she can muster, she produces a critique of the Bible that is at once a critique of the cultures that read it.

In *The Nakedness of the Fathers*, Ostriker places herself in several traditions at once – an American women's tradition of biblical critique dating back at least to Sarah Grimke's *Letters on the Equality of the Sexes and the Condition of Woman* (1838), together with a twentieth-century tradition of women's rewritings of the Bible that includes, for instance, Zora Neale Hurston's *Moses Man of the Mountain* and Jeannette Winterson's *Boating for Beginners*. And she attaches herself to the Jewish tradition of midrash which she defines as 'stories based on Biblical stories, composed not for a narrow audience of scholars and legalists, but for the entire community. Through midrash, ancient tales yield new meanings to new generations' (*NF*, Preface). Additionally, she joins the midrash tradition of Jewish feminism, an attempt to liberate Torah's positive meanings for women, to make biblical scholarship the work of all the Jewish people (instead of only half of them, as Cynthia Ozick observes), and, in some cases, as Judith Plaskow recommends, to balance the biblical god by including the goddess.[16]

Ostriker's work is also part of the women's spirituality movement which has engaged an array of thinkers both within and without Judaism in the task of rewriting religion in the light of women's experiences and desires. Reforming religion involves these women in working for the end of what Mary Daly calls 'rapism', the system of patriarchal racism and colonialism they believe to be nourished by male-oriented religion.[17] For some writers, such as Gloria Anzaldua and Paula Gunn Allen, the movement involves a return to the spiritual ways of their subjugated ancestors.[18] Central to women's spirituality is the restoration of the goddess presumed to have been obliterated by male monotheism. In Ostriker's rewriting, the biblical god swallows the goddess, and, in his death scene at the end, he is grotesquely in labor with her rebirth. The book ends with 'A Closing Prayer', a poem announcing the triumphal return of the goddess: 'On that day will our God be One / And their name One.'

In her rewriting of the Bible, Ostriker continues to take part in white feminism's struggle to correct its elitism thanks to being forcibly educated by sister-outsiders. Although a few white poets are the backbone of *Stealing the Language*, leaving us with a sense of a white center to the movement, Ostriker is careful to point out the diversity of women's experience because to ignore this diversity is to claim that, in Hull, Scott, and Smith's famous phrase, 'all the women are white'.[19] Thus, she tries to include a range of poets differing from one another by race, ethnicity, sexual orientation, and class. In *The Nakedness of the Fathers*, her treatment of biblical connections to history reaches out across race, class, and national lines. She recognizes difference by problematizing divisions among women arising from their separate places in the matrix of domination. For instance, being women together does not give Sarah and Hagar a community of interest. Difference also enters into her appropriation of Chloe and Olivia, those new working-women heroines of fiction invented by Virginia Woolf in *A Room of One's Own*, whom Ostriker separates by race and class, giving the woman of color the last word about the death of god and the birth of the goddess – 'Well, burn my bush' – a comment that may indicate her Mosaic role in the new order (IC, p. 36).

*The Nakedness of the Fathers* makes multiple contributions to literary theory. Most obviously it reforms biblical myths, accounts for the disappearance of women from the Bible and western culture, and replaces the masculine hero-quest as the ultimate mythical narrative with what Ostriker calls 'the mama–papa story'. It also demonstrates the myriad possibilities in texts: the final liberatory message of literature is multiplicity and continuum, not dichotomy – 'everything that lives is holy'. It reveals the continuity between literature and life by connecting the Bible with daily life, family, journalism, politics, crisis centers, wars, racial oppression, and much else. It shows reading, analysis, and creation each to be the products of desire, imagination, and identity. It asserts the role of literature in cultural critique and culture formation and reformation. (As Claire R. Satloff says of Jewish feminist fiction, it is 'not just another literary occurrence, but an attempt at new Jewish culture-making'.[20]) *The Nakedness of the Fathers* is a work of creative reading as liberation, asserting that oppressed groups can find life-giving sources in literature and culture, neither of which is monolithic. Most of all, the work is a demonstration of a whole woman reading, a product of history and culture, grounded in late twentieth-century America – a Jew, mother, teacher, daughter, granddaughter, wife, anti-war protestor, inheritor and bequeather of history.

*The Nakedness of the Fathers* harks back to one of the foundation documents of feminist literary criticism, Virginia Woolf's *A Room of One's Own*, which conveys its ideas through an elaborate fiction of the author's two-day search for an understanding of the subject 'women and fiction', complete with trenchant and entertaining metaphors for patriarchal exclusion of women. Many feminists strive for a similar style, a voice that is, in Carol Christ's words, 'passionate, personal, political *and* scholarly, and reflective'.[21] Such a style reintroduces the pleasure principle into criticism. It responds to literature by speaking the same language – the language that originally drew the critic and theorist into literary studies. As a language for literary theory and criticism, metaphor and narrative reach out, permeate boundaries, find

correspondences. Articulating theory in the language of
literature, of dream, and of imagination, which may very
well be the sites of its creation, is a refusal to ape an
objectivity and tidiness we don't possess, opting instead
for accessibility and emotion. As Ostriker says in 'Entering the Tents', 'Reader, my case is like yours, perhaps.
Perhaps yours is like mine. A case of (some kind of)
love' (ET, p. 543).

**Catherine Pastore Blair**

> *Does the unanswered prayer*
> *Corrode the tissue of heaven*
>
> *Doesn't it rust the wings*
> *Of the heavenly host . . .*

Alicia Ostriker, 'A Meditation in Seven Days'

As Alice Jardine has observed, 'At this point it seems
impossible to think difference without thinking it ag-
gressively or defensively. But think we must, because if
we don't it will continue to think us, as it has since
Genesis at the very least.'[22] With the same sense of an
historical necessity, Ostriker presents in this book Jardine's
two possibilities: a patriarchal text 'thinking us' in the
first lecture and us 'thinking difference' in the second,
the disappearance of woman in biblical narratives and
woman's spiritual re-emergence in modern and contemporary verse. As in *Stealing the Language*, female identity
is itself the core and cause of a poetics whose authority
is historical necessity rather than aesthetic confirmation

of an already established canonical taste. What is implied in Ostriker's fierce advocacy of the phenomenology of a female voice thus attempts not to alter the canon 'slightly' and thereby not to to change it, as Eliot would have had it, and as some of Ostriker's critics would have advised, but to propose a more radical alternative.

The elegist of Ostriker's splendid 'A Meditation in Seven Days' will attempt neither the 'words addressed to an atomic father', nor the emotional distance of (male) 'speculation', nor the self-validating 'wisdom of the wise' if only

> so that suddenly
> Our human grief illuminated, we're a circle
>
> Practical and magical.

The historical and ahistorical dimensions of Ostriker's spiritual desire intersect in the figure of the mother lighting the Sabbath candles. The light that Ostriker hopes to wrest from the Bible appears similarly at the moment of imminent initiation into an unprecedented historical and spiritual aperture: the poem's last lines fearfully announce a hand 'on the latch / I am the woman, and about to enter.' Though the door is only ajar, and one can't see much more than 'a square of blue sky', one thing – such fearfulness suggests – is clear: a daughter's entrance into a father's tent is the apt metaphor for the political, economic, spiritual passage women have sought and have been denied, the passage being defended as it always is with moral prohibitions and with notions of sexual unseemliness.

As in *Stealing the Language*, in the present lectures Ostriker insists with eloquence and moral urgency that the strongest argument for the viability of an emerging female spirituality is to point out its existence. If *Stealing the Language* is an informative, thought-provoking account of female responses to patriarchy, such a phenomenology points out how 'women poets are in the process of transforming the thematic landscape of our language', or, as one of Ostriker's commentators, Frieda Gardner, goes on to say, how 'a great variety of women poets are saying things that have never been said before'.[23]

Biblical revisionism is as old as Genesis. Equally ancient, if systematically suppressed and silenced, has been woman's claim to change 'the indictment served on her in Paradise'. The irony and phrase are from Elizabeth Cady Stanton, who notes in *The Woman's Bible* (1895) that 'when, in the early part of the Nineteenth Century, women began to protest against their civil and political degradation, they were referred to the Bible for an answer.'[24] As with Stanton, who rebelled against the 'impress of fallible man' in the Bible and yet attempted to regain a vision of 'our ideal first great cause' through the same text, Ostriker's reading of the Bible is inspired both by a radical critique of its patriarchal ideology and by her hope to 'wrest a blessing' from it – nevertheless (p. 86). Such a twofold purpose, marrying as it does the secular to the sacred, is implied in Ostriker's tracing of a divine (d) origin sheltered from the unholy writ of history: 'Woman and man are alike, at the very beginning' (ET, p. 546). But can one bind together, can one *re-ligare*, what in the ensuing biblical narrative is so disastrously put asunder?

Like Ostriker's 'very beginning', which is markedly different from the usual accounts of the origins of Man, Phyllis Trible, in her meticulous textual archeology in *God and the Rhetoric of Sexuality* (1978), seeks to divulge an origin beyond the hierarchies of gendered difference.[25] Although Trible's intention is to reveal a sexual commensurability inscribed as a pre-lapsarian 'unity, solidarity, mutuality and equality', she also discovers duality, hierarchy, duplicity: a slight textual partiality towards the woman who is 'unique in creation' because she is 'built of raw material from the earth creature rather than from the earth'. Yet a few pages later Trible demurs: 'the rib is raw material, comparable to dust from the earth'. But this is taken back when she restates that 'She is unique. Unlike the rest of creation, she does not come from the earth'. In *Lethal Love* (1987), Mieke Bal repeats Trible's argument as well as her partiality. She draws attention to 'two progressive phases of perfection' which, she holds, prove Paul's 'mistake': 'The material that is used no longer consists of dust, of clay, but of bone and flesh, already enriched with *nepes*. The result is also higher: it is . . . a woman.'[26] However, as Gerda Lerner insists, 'there is little evidence in other parts of the Bible to support these optimistically feminist interpretations.'[27]

Lerner's sobering advice suggests an irreparable belatedness in our attempts to recover a more equitable text. In the course of the biblical narrative, Ostriker points out, 'the penis, that flexible flesh, hardens into the metal of the sword' (ET, p. 546). In spite of such forbidding allegories of Scripture, for Ostriker its very textuality is capable of subverting the Bible's 'violently masculine' (*GA*, p. 46) intentions. For the language of the Bible has unmeant meanings. One commentator has rightly pointed out that Ostriker's feminist stance 'is informed by recent French theorists like Derrida, Lacan and their female students'.[28] But these are affinities rather than affiliations. They account nevertheless for an influence that is appreciably present in this book, when the Bible is described as 'a radically layered, plurally authored, multiply motivated composite, full of fascinating mysteries, gaps, and inconsistencies, a garden of delight . . . a kind of paradise of polysemy' (p. 62). Consequently, to 'posit a simple polarity or adversarial relationship between male text and female re/writers' would be to find oneself East of this textual Eden, in the position of the exiled, fallen female from which she would speak as either the envious commentator or the disinherited bystander. Rather than to assume such an implicitly reverential or defeated position, Ostriker keeps and tills her textual garden to watch it grow what has always already been there, albeit muted and female. 'If the Bible is a flaming sword forbidding our entrance to the garden,' Ostriker concludes in these lectures, 'it is also a burning bush urging us toward freedom' (p. 86).

Indeed, one might add, if the patriarchs' pleasure had required a garden of stone, a monolith of textual rigidity, why the story of the shattering of Moses' tablets of stone? And why the rewriting by the hand of Moses of what was first written by the finger of God? And why that allegory of textual opacity in Moses' veil on his descent from Mount Sinai? Why the rhetoric of narrative artificiality in Job's frame-story? Or why, as Frank Kermode has put it, the boy in the shirt?[29] Roland Barthes has eloquently pointed out that such a plural text demands to be not pierced but traversed, not deciphered but disentangled.[30]

Yet 'a tangle of sandy footprints' announces 'another story'. In the unpunctuated movements of Ostriker's 'A Meditation in Seven Days', irony and invocation, elegy and eloquence are availed to reconstitute a still more inclusive plurality. While for Barthes the plural, writerly text results benevolently 'from a thousand sources of culture', for Ostriker the Bible's repressive un-writing of the female narrative has effectively diminished a thousandfold potential. This, in turn, forces Ostriker not only to traverse but to pierce her cultural heritage: 'I must confront what is toxic – but I must also do more than that' (p. 30). Scripture thus survives as a potential for cultural and spiritual rejuvenation only because the repressions are too obsessively repeated and too imperfectly erased. Her initial announcement that she would 'not posit a simple polarity or adversarial relationship

between male text and female re/writers' (p. 28) finds
itself thus revised retrospectively: in the second lecture
she admits to having held an 'adversarial' stance towards
the Bible (p 56). This theoretical volatility does not,
however, come entirely by surprise. Ostriker's entire
project appears under the sign of a cultural and spiritual
paradox, a double loyalty, as Catherine Blair points out
in the first part of this introduction. Ostriker's urge 'to
freedom' is pursued in spite of the 'flaming sword' of
the biblical text, her desire for a 'blessing' is by 'demand', her striving 'toward wholeness' is within the frac-
tures of her self.

In his essay on the Book of Esther, Richard Howard
reports the disappearance of Vashti, who is to Howard's
'obstinate hypothesis, one of those haunting, secret
figures in literature, like Lot's wife, who make one de-
cisive negative gesture, who violate a commandment and
then vanish forever, leaving only a symbolic transgression for memorial'.[31] In this book Ostriker argues that
female identity *itself* constitutes historically and cultur-
ally such a transgression, and that the memorial has to
be written and has been written, as she documents in
*Stealing the Language*, by scores of women poets. In her
own example from *Green Age*: woman

> is unclean in her sex, . . . she is
> Created to be a defilement and a temptation
>
> A snake with breasts like a female
> A succubus, a flying vagina
>
> So that the singing of God
> The secret of God
>
> The name winged in the hues of the rainbow
> Is withheld from her.
>
> (*GA*, p. 48)

The Bible, Ostriker argues, conceals, but reveals as it conceals, a collective repression of the female – a theory which she convincingly appropriates for her very different purposes from Freud's essay *Moses and Monotheism*. Freud's theory allows her, likewise, to read in the biblical text the language of a cultural unconscious wherein she discovers imperfectly erased traces of female presence both divine and mortal. 'Inside the oldest stories are older stories', she writes in a recent essay, 'not destroyed but hidden. Swallowed. Mouth songs. Nobody knows how many. The texts retain traces, leakages, lacunae, curious figures of speech, jagged irruptions' (ET, p. 547). As a feminist, Ostriker's desire to re-present forgotten presences – Sarah and Miriam are remembered in the first lecture – is also the desire to re-member and reconstitute herself from the very cultural *bricolage* and linguistic gaps which allow forbidden entrances into the father's tent: 'What if I say these traces too are mine?' (ET, p. 547).

Ostriker discovers in the biblical narrative what Freud discovered in jokes, parapraxes, and dreams: a 'startlingly recurrent pattern' (p. 49) of symbolic, subliminal traces – of woman. But so deeply repressed is this textual unconscious,[32] so well forgotten are Sarah and Miriam, that the triumph of patriarchy cannot but belie the complexity and plurality of the Bible's language. Thus, what emerges as a result of Ostriker's critique is that patriarchal suppression of the female actually limits the inexhaustible meanings of Scripture, thwarting the Bible's pluralistic textuality, levelling its radical layering.

To restore just those complexities and those diviner and more artistic intentions, Ostriker turns in her second lecture to the poetic imagination as a transgressive force and to the Bible once again, this time as a record of repeated instances of transgression. The profoundest and spiritually most potent example of the Bible's textual heterodoxy occurs, perhaps paradoxically, in Ostriker's notion of the Bible as 'intrinsically no more absolute in its authority than other writing' (p. 61), for only as such could the Bible engender the self-revising continuity that Ostriker attributes to its lasting influence.

Her examples range from the biblical text itself (for that empowers the subsequent poetic imagination), to Emily Dickinson, Elizabeth Barrett Browning, Christina Rossetti, H. D., and contemporary American women poets, whose theologically subversive strategies enlarge the biblical canon. That these are all women seems at first sight incidental, since Ostriker appears intent on granting the privilege of slipping through patriarchal loopholes not to the female but to the poetic imagination. As in *Stealing the Language*, the poets she quotes thus appropriate what appears as an already generically proven tool of cultural revision. But aesthetic subversion has been absorbed in our culture like those legendary leopards whose nightly interruptions of a religious ritual were eventually incorporated in the ritual itself. Hence Ostriker's insistence, both here as well as in *Stealing the Language*, on a *thematically* different kind of writing – exemplified in 'The Lilith Poems'.

The most immediate literary and spiritual predecessor of Ostriker's Lilith is the mysterious 'Lady' in H. D.'s 'Tribute to the Angels'. Like Lilith, H. D.'s Lady 'is no symbolic figure / of peace, charity, chastity, goodness, / faith, hope, reward'.[33] To speak in the voice of Lilith – which is, in Ostriker's rendition, to speak in the voice of a black woman – suggests that, like H. D., Ostriker wishes to bind together, to *re-ligare*, Barthes's thousand sources of culture, so that (in H. D.'s words) 'her book is our book; written / or unwritten'. Not only does Lilith take up her abode with wolves and satyrs, as well as with gods and men, but Lilith, as Harold Bloom has suggested, is also a reminder of what we have forgotten: 'a column left alone of a temple once complete'.[34]

The poetic passages in Ostriker's second lecture seek to reconstruct the temple from the ruins of our culture.

Rather than dwell on individual architectural designs and their aesthetic pleasures ('the trick of the pen or brush,' as H. D. mocks), Ostriker has pointed out that her project is to represent not the poetic genre but 'a literary movement', whose 'thematic choices may generate nonnormative stylistic decisions', and that 'such writing enlarges what we mean by literature and humanity'.[35] Although such large intentions may violate the aesthetic integrity of the individual poem, Ostriker's example in her first lecture – Rukeyser's retelling of the riddle of the Sphinx from the point of view of woman – seems sufficiently to justify her choices, and with not a small scandal. The scandal, even if not perceived as such by those who belittle its significance, is that Oedipus' answer to the Sphinx did not include woman. This leads Ostriker to the observation that there might be a more 'substantial relation' between the Sphinx as a figure of 'pre-patriarchal female power' and Oedipus' 'tragic doom' (p. 29) than a male consciousness would have allowed. Yet, even if the inclusion of woman might offer fundamental new insights, some of Ostriker's critics fear that though the insights might teach they might not delight.

Ostriker has made her position on aesthetic significance clear in an article in *Critical Inquiry*: 'Any poetry which is merely political – and nothing else – is shallow poetry' (DDP, p. 585). Some of her reviewers claim that she fails to apply such a principle to the poetic examples in *Stealing the Language*. Similar charges might be levelled against some of Ostriker's poetic examples in this book. Bonnie Costello, who would have liked Ostriker to affirm 'the possibility of the universal in art', accuses her of being 'defensive', and deplores 'Ostriker's underestimation of the greats' and 'her indifference to questions of quality'.[36] Liz Rosenberg regrets that Ostriker is not interested in such 'aesthetic' questions as: 'is [the poetry] musical, beautiful, lush, spare, intelligent, fair-minded? How do women's line breaks work?'[37] Mary Karr demands that Ostriker submit to 'the rigor' of aesthetic judgment, that she synthesize 'moral concerns with aesthetic ones'.[38] Karr's somewhat revealing metaphor of 'Ostriker's failure to woo her readers with such rigor' may stand as representative for these critics' unconscious investments of aesthetic delight with moral force – an investment precisely that Ostriker seeks to question with her thematic choices. Even if Ostriker's or anyone else's 'moral concern' here as elsewhere cannot be sufficient unto itself (though such faculties have been ascribed to the aesthetic), the sudden vigor with which some critics hope for a more equitable world, if only the rigor of aesthetics were more mercilessly applied, is astounding. The dialogic opponent of H. D.'s visionary in 'Tribute to the Angels' assumes the aesthetic perspective of these critics when she (or he) proclaims the Lady 'as symbol of beauty':

> flanked by Corinthian capitals,
> or in a Coptic nave,
>
> or frozen above the centre door
> of a Gothic cathedral.

However, cultural change and literary innovation have never, to my knowledge, come about by virtue of 'formal and thematic rigor' (as recommended by one of Ostriker's critics)[39] but rather by aesthetic aberrations such as Eliot's patient etherized upon a table, or Lowell's daddy booming in his bathtub, or Plath's skin bright as a Nazi lampshade. H. D. envisions her Lady 'not / imprisoned in leaden bars / in a coloured window' but in 'the unwritten volume of the new'.

**Harold Schweizer**

REFERENCES

The following works by Alicia Ostriker are cited in the Introduction:

*Vision and Verse in William Blake* (Madison: University of Wisconsin Press, 1965) (*VV*)

*Writing Like a Woman* (Ann Arbor: University of Michigan Press, 1983) (*WW*)

*Stealing the Language: The Emergence of Women's Poetry in America* (Boston: Beacon Press, 1986) (*SL*)

'Dancing at the Devil's Party: Some Notes on Politics and Poetry', *Critical Inquiry* 13, no. 3 (Spring 1987), pp. 579–96 (DDP)

'Intensive Care', *Santa Monica Review* 1, no. 1 (Fall 1988), pp. 31–6 (IC)

*Green Age* (Pittsburgh: University of Pittsburgh Press, 1989) (*GA*)

'Comment on Claire Kahane: Questioning the Maternal Voice', *Genders* 4 (March 1989), pp. 130–3 (CCK)

'Entering the Tents', *Feminist Studies* 15, no. 3 (Fall 1989), pp. 541–7 (ET)

'The Road of Excess: My William Blake', in *The Romantics and Us: Essays on Romantic and Modern Culture*, ed. Gene W. Ruoff (New Brunswick, NJ: Rutgers University Press, 1990), pp. 67–88 (RE)

'The Wisdom of Solomon', *Kenyon Review* 12, no. 2 (Spring 1990), pp. 149–55 (WS)

*The Nakedness of the Fathers: A Woman Reading the Bible* (forthcoming) (*NF*)

NOTES

1 Elaine Showalter, 'Women's Time, Women's Space: Writing the History of Feminist Criticism', in *Feminist Issues in Literary Scholarship*, ed. Shari Benstock (Bloomington: Indiana University Press, 1987), p. 37.

2   Josephine Donovan, 'Toward a Women's Poetics', in Benstock, p. 100.

3   At least three reviewers of *Stealing the Language* take Ostriker to task for lack of 'standards': Bonnie Costello, 'Writing Like a Woman', *Contemporary Literature* 29, no. 2 (1988), pp. 305–10; Mary Karr, 'Sexual Poetics', *Poetry* 149 (Fall 1987), pp. 294–303; Liz Rosenberg, 'The Power of Victims', *New York Times*, 20 July 1986, p. 21.

4   Jane Gallop, 'Heroic Images: Feminist Criticism, 1972', *American Literary History* 1, no. 3 (Fall 1989), pp. 620–4.

5   Nina Auerbach, 'Engorging the Patriarchy', in Benstock, p. 152.

6   Donna Haraway, 'A Manifesto for Cyborgs: Science, Technology, and Socialist Feminism in the 1980s', in *Feminism/Postmodernism*, ed. Linda J. Nicholson (New York: Routledge, 1990), p. 199.

7   Elaine Showalter, 'Women's Time, Women's Space', p. 41.

8   Nina Baym, 'The Madwoman and Her Languages: Why I Don't Do Feminist Literary Theory', in Benstock, p. 55.

9   Patricia Hill Collins, *Black Feminist Thought* (Boston: Unwin Hyman, 1990), p. xii.

10  Portions of the book quoted here have been cited in unpublished MS form except for 'Entering the Tents', 'The Wisdom of Solomon', and 'Intensive Care', which have been published and are therefore cited in their published versions.

11  Rachel Blau DuPlessis, 'For the Etruscans', in *The New Feminist Criticism*, ed. Elaine Showalter (New York: Pantheon Books, 1985), p. 276.

12  Patrocinio P. Schweickart, 'Reading Ourselves: Toward a Feminist Theory of Reading', in *Gender and Reading*, eds Elizabeth A. Flynn and Patrocinio P. Schweickart (Baltimore: Johns Hopkins University Press, 1986), pp. 43–4.

13  Alice Walker, *In Search of Our Mothers' Gardens* (New York: Harcourt Brace Jovanovich, 1983), p. xi.

14  Nina Auerbach, 'Engorging the Patriarchy', in Benstock, pp. 150–60.

15 Adrienne Rich, 'When We Dead Awaken: Writing as Re-Vision', in *On Lies, Secrets, and Silence* (New York: W. W. Norton, 1979), p. 35.

16 Cynthia Ozick, 'Notes Toward Finding the Right Question', in *On Being a Jewish Feminist*, ed. Susannah Heschel (New York: Schocken Books, 1983), p. 138; Judith Plaskow, 'The Right Question is Theological', in Heschel, pp. 229–30.

17 Mary Daly, *Beyond God the Father: Toward a Philosophy of Women's Liberation* (Boston: Beacon Press, 1985), p. xvi.

18 Paula Gunn Allen, *The Sacred Hoop: Recovering the Feminine in American Indian Traditions* (Boston: Beacon Press, 1986); Gloria Anzaldua, *Borderlands/La Frontera: The New Mestiza* (San Francisco: Spinsters/Aunt Lute Book Company, 1987).

19 *(All the Women Are White, All the Blacks Are Men) But Some of Us Are Brave*, eds Gloria T. Hull, Patricia Bell Scott, and Barbara Smith (New York: Feminist Press, 1982).

20 Claire R. Satloff, 'History, Fiction, and Tradition: Creating a Jewish Feminist Poetic', in Heschel, p. 199.

21 Carol Christ, *Diving Deep and Surfacing: Women Writers on Spiritual Quest*, 2nd edn (Boston: Beacon Press, 1986), p. xi.

22 *The Future of Difference*, eds Hester Eisenstein and Alice Jardine (Boston: G. K. Hall and Co., 1980), p. xxvi.

23 Frieda Gardner, 'From Masters to Muses', *The Woman's Review of Books* 4, no. 7 (April 1987), p. 14.

24 Elizabeth Cady Stanton, *The Woman's Bible* (New York: European Publishing Company, 1895), pp. 8, 13.

25 Phyllis Trible, *God and the Rhetoric of Sexuality* (Philadelphia: Fortress Press, 1978), p. 18. Subsequent references in this paragraph are to pp. 96, 99, 100, 102.

26 Mieke Bal, *Lethal Love* (Bloomington: Indiana University Press, 1987), pp. 115–16.

27 Gerda Lerner, *The Creation of Patriarchy* (New York: Oxford University Press, 1986), p. 184.

28 Cheryl Walker, Review of *Stealing the Language*, in *Signs* 14, no. 1 (Autumn 1988), p. 220.

29 Cf. Frank Kermode's chapter with that title in *The Genesis of Secrecy: On the Interpretation of Narrative* (Cambridge,

Mass.: Harvard University Press, 1979), where the figure (from the Gospel of Mark) allegorizes the inexhaustible mysteries of a literary text.

30   Roland Barthes, 'The Death of the Author', in *The Rustle of Language*, tr. Richard Howard (New York: Hill & Wang, 1986), pp. 53–4.

31   Richard Howard, 'Apart: Hearing Secret Harmonies', in *Congregation: Contemporary Writers Read the Jewish Bible*, ed. David Rosenberg (New York: Harcourt Brace Jovanovich, 1987), p. 410.

32   In *Totem and Taboo* (IV, 6) Freud briefly mentions the possibility of a female goddess (*Muttergottheit*) that might have preceded the male god. But the oedipal structure of his inquiry into the origins of religion admits no space for a goddess. Similarly Julia Kristeva, in 'Stabat Mater', speaks of Freud's collection of 'innumerable statuettes of mother goddesses. Yet in the work of the founder of psychoanalysis this interest is alluded to only discreetly': *Contemporary Critical Theory*, ed. Dan Latimer (New York: Harcourt Brace Jovanovich, 1989), p. 595.

33   H. D., *Trilogy* (New York: New Directions, 1973), section 39. Subsequent quotations are from this edition: sections 37, 38, 40.

34   Harold Bloom, *Figures of Capable Imagination* (New York: The Seabury Press, 1976), p. 265.

35   'Response to Bonnie Costello', *Contemporary Literature* 30, no. 3 (1989), pp. 462, 464.

36   Bonnie Costello, 'Writing Like a Woman', pp. 306, 308.

37   Liz Rosenberg, 'The Power of Victims', p. 21.

38   Mary Karr, 'Sexual Poetics', p. 302.

39   Bonnie Costello, 'Response to Alicia Ostriker', *Contemporary Literature* 30, no. 3 (1989), p. 467.

# Out of my Sight: The Buried Woman in Biblical Narrative

What if the book were only infinite memory of a word
lacking?

> Edmund Jabès, *Adam, or the Birth of Anxiety*[1]

Somewhere every culture has an imaginary zone for what
it excludes, and it is that zone which we must try to
remember today.

> Catherine Clément, *The Newly Born Woman*[2]

What happens when women re-imagine culture? What is
the relation of the female writer to the male text, the male
story? How can we – how do we – deal with that ur-text
of patriarchy, that particular set of canonized tales from
which our theory and practice of canonicity derives, that
paradigmatic meta-narrative in which innumerable small
narratives rest like many eggs in a very large basket – the
Book of Books which we call the Bible? How shall
women, as Mieke Bal asks in *Lethal Love: Feminist Literary Readings of Biblical Love Stories*, 'rewrite themselves
back into the history of ideology'?[3] And how, where, do
I locate myself with respect to the looming male tradition of religion, myth, philosophy, and literature?

I take these questions to be a single question, to which
I will not give a conventional 'feminist' answer. That is

to say: I will not posit a simple polarity or adversarial relationship between male text and female re/writers. In the final chapter of my book *Stealing the Language: The Emergence of Women's Poetry in America*, I found myself unable to accept the notion of a purely feminine language or a purely female literary tradition. Looking at revisionist mythmaking by contemporary women poets, I posited that all myths central to a culture survive through a process of continual reinterpretation, satisfying the contradictory needs of individuals and society for images and narratives of both continuity and transformation. I argued that vital myths are paradoxically both public and private, that they encode both consent to and dissent from existing power structures, and that they have at all times a potential for being interpreted both officially and subversively. In that book I proposed women writers' revisionist versions of classical myths as an invasion of the sanctuaries of existing language, the treasuries where our meanings for 'male' and 'female' are preserved.[4] A brief example: Muriel Rukeyser's 'Myth' recounts an unrecorded conversation between Oedipus and the Sphinx. Old and blind, Oedipus wants to know where he went wrong, and the Sphinx explains that he answered her famous question incorrectly:

'When I asked, What walks on four legs in the morning, two at noon, and three in the evening, you answered, Man. You didn't say anything about woman.'
'When you say Man,' said Oedipus, 'you include women too. Everyone knows that.' She said, 'That's what you think.'

Let me note in passing several strategies of the revisionist woman poet which this tiny poem exemplifies. First, and most obviously, the female poet gives voice to female silence. Second, and appositely, she brackets

a question of language; in this case, the poem draws
attention to the male-gendered universal. To theorize
this strategy is to observe that conventions of grammar
form a ubiquitous though usually unacknowledged
source of women's oppression. Third, the poet finds
something *in* the myth which nobody noticed before,
and which only a woman would be likely to notice: a
possible substantial (not merely accidental) relation between the tragic hero's original encounter with a figure
representing archaic, pre-Greek, pre-patriarchal female
power, and his tragic doom. Where a masculinist reading fails to connect the Oedipus–Sphinx episode with
the later Oedipal tragedy, a feminist reading makes precisely that connection; and it is typical of women's
rewriting of myth that, when meanings already latent
in a given story are recovered and foregrounded by a
woman's perspective, the entire story appears to change.
But perhaps we should not say the story changes. Perhaps we should merely say that it grows. Fourth, and I
think this is the feature of female revisionism which
scholars find most irritating and which I consider essential to the work of feminism, the feminist poet replays
tragedy as farce. What is supposed to be sacred becomes
a joke. And I believe that whatever is sacred *must*
become, somehow or other, a joke, if we want to free
ourselves of mental tyranny. For laughter, the 'scourge
of tyrants', is the most revolutionary weapon in literature's arsenal. We all remember Wallace Stevens's
poem poking fun at the moral law of the 'High-Toned
Old Christian Woman', reminding her that 'fictive
things / Wink as they will. Wink most when widows
wince'. Well, when traditional humanists wince at feminist comedy, thinking it silly, or strident, or whatever,
comedy winks back. The laugh of the Sphinx, like the
laugh of the Medusa, is the cackle/chuckle of the silenced
woman finding her voice. Not at all silly, not at all
hysterical.

My present writing is an extension of my work in *Stealing the Language*. As critic and poet, as Jew, woman and (dare I say) human being, I am involved in a collective enterprise which has as its ultimate goal the radical transformation of what used to be called 'the Judeo-Christian tradition'. Yet my quest springs directly from the core of that tradition and is the inevitable consequence of it. I have become saturated in what the poet H. D., whose late writing constitutes an attempt to unify Egyptian, Greek and Christian mythos, called 'spiritual realism'. In other words, I am engaged both theoretically and practically in the question of what will happen when the spiritual imagination of women, women who may call themselves Jews or Christians, pagans or atheists, witches or worshippers of the Great Goddess, is released into language and into history. Let me emphasize here that I do not want to separate what I do as a scholar and critic from what I do as a poet, nor do I wish to divide my writing from my life, or my intellect from my passions or my spirituality. The entire weight of western thought commands that I do so; to the best of my ability I will resist that command. I will try to think and write myself toward wholeness, by which I mean integration of plurality. This is not to say that I claim to have or to be a 'unitary self'. Far from it, I feel desperately fractured much of the time, as anyone in a pathological culture must. But I strive for healing. And so I must confront what is toxic – but I must also do more than that.

In my first lecture I will argue, as provocatively as I can, that the biblical story of monotheism and covenant is, to use the language of politics, a cover-up; that when we lift the cover we find quite another story, an obsessively told and retold story of erased female power. Biblical patriarchy, as I see it, figuratively encodes within its text the repeated acts of literal murder and oppression necessary for its triumph. That is not *all* it does, in my opinion; but I hope to convince you that it does do that. By extension, I would argue that the canonizing process throughout our history has rested, not accidentally but essentially, on the silencing of women. But in my second lecture I will argue first that these same canonized biblical texts, and the traditions built on them, encourage and even invite transgressive as well as orthodox readings; then that the outrageous rewritings of biblical narrative by women poets, far from destroying sacred Scripture, are designed to revitalize it and make it sacred indeed to that half of the human population which has been degraded by it.

My premise throughout is that, as the rabbis have long told us, 'there is always another interpretation.' If biblical interpretation until the present moment has been virtually exclusively the prerogative of males, so much the more reason for women to make a beginning. 'Turn it and turn it,' the rabbis say of Torah, 'for everything is in it.' As the poet Adrienne Rich long ago asserted, 'Re-vision – the act of looking back, of seeing with fresh eyes, of entering an old text from a new critical direction – is for women more than a chapter in cultural history; it is an act of survival.'[5] The truths of women, then, along with the truths of men. Our tragic losses, but also, perhaps, our divine comedy.

I

Let me begin my discussion of burial with that most provocative of biblical exegetes, Freud, who in *Moses and Monotheism* proposes that biblical tradition results from two opposing desires among redactors: to keep a sacred text piously unchanged regardless of inconsistencies, and to transform the text according to present needs. 'The distortion of a text is not unlike a murder', Freud famously remarks. 'The difficulty lies not in the execution of the deed but in the doing away with the traces.' When disparate traditions coalesce, Freud claims, 'the repressed material retains its impetus to penetrate into consciousness', and does so when resistance is diminished, i.e. when the ego is 'ill or asleep'; when instincts attached to repressed material are strengthened, as in puberty; or when recent events parallel repressed ones and awaken them.[6] Freud's aim in *Moses and Monotheism* is to prove that Moses was an Egyptian, that Judaism as we know it comes from the coalescence of a residual Egyptian monotheism with indigenous Canaanite worship of a volcano-god, and that Moses was assassinated by his followers, who then repressed the memory of his assassination. It is this repression which in Freud's view largely accounts for the subsequent energy of Judaism.

In the course of his argument Freud makes, almost incidentally, another observation. Noting that a key attribute of the monotheism of the Israelites as against the polytheism of their neighbors was its prohibition against images, he links this prohibition with the triumph of patriarchy. For, where maternity is a physically determinable fact, paternity remains an inference. The father-principle is that-which-must-be-deduced, an intellectual substance, as against the mother who is all too evident to the senses. A dematerialized Heavenly Father is a further step away from the Earthly Mother. Thus, in Freud's scenario, patriarchal monotheism, 'subordinating sense perception to an abstract idea . . . was a triumph of spirituality over the senses'.[7]

Might, in this formulation, is conveniently also right. The Father is not merely stronger, he is also *spiritually superior* to the Mother. Absence and abstraction are spiritually superior to presence and physicality – for reasons never quite stated, which a mere woman may find difficult to understand. Thereby, of course, hangs the philosophical tale of all patriarchal culture, whether pagan or Judeo-Christian.

Subsequent biblical and Near Eastern studies have failed to document Freud's theory of Moses' Egyptian origin or of his assassination. They have, on the other hand, massively confirmed the second murder gestured at by *Moses and Monotheism*: Judaism's replacement of indigenous polytheisms by the One God of the Israelites, who absorbed important features of earlier deities including their maternal powers, while at the same time the existence of these other gods was denied and their worship forbidden. The monotheism of Judaism, Christianity, and Islam extends, in fact, an aeons-long shift in the conception of divinity. As Raphael Patai synopsizes:

> The earliest answers to the great question of 'Whence' all reiterate, in various forms, the same idea: it was out of the body of the primordial goddess that the world-egg emerged or that the earth was born; or alternately, it was the goddess' body itself that provided the material from which the earth was made.[8]

Statues of Near Eastern goddesses can be dated to 25,000 BC, millennia prior to any male gods. From the fourth millennium forward, written records in the form of myths, rituals, and creation stories confirm the priority of female divinity. Priority, however, does not guarantee supremacy. Rather, the major creation myths of the ancient world encode the overthrow of goddess-worshipping cultures. Gerda Lerner summarizes the transition to worship of dominantly male pantheons:

> The observable pattern is: first, the demotion of the Mother-Goddess figure and the ascendance and later dominance of her male consort/son; then his merging with a storm-god into a male Creator-God, who heads

the pantheon of gods and goddesses. Whenever such changes occur, the power of creation and fertility is transferred from the Goddess to the God.[9]

J. A. Phillips observes the connection between the demotion of the female principle from dominance to domesticity and the conception of culture in mythic narrative:

> The great creation stories of ancient Near Eastern cultures have at least two important things in common: All deal with the initiation and sustenance of human civilization, the securing of religious and cosmological foundations for the *polis*; and all presuppose or describe power struggles between masculine and feminine deities, usually with the masculine deities gaining the upper hand. It is as though the writers believed that civilization could not begin or be sustained until the Feminine, as a dominant religious power, had been mastered and domesticated.[10]

Ancient writing prior to the advent of monotheism consistently recalls the primordial past in a context of violent transition. In the Mesopotamian creation-epic *Enuma Elish*, the warrior-god Marduk defeats the dragon-mother-goddess Tiamat, and forms the cosmos from her split carcass. In Canaanite myth, the paternal warrior-god El defeats both his parents and marries his two sisters. In Hesiod's *Theogony*, the jealous Ouranos pushes his infant sons back into the womb of Gaia; Kronos castrates Ouranos and swallows his own progeny lest they overthrow him; the once-powerful goddesses Gaia and Rheia suffer submissively. Zeus in turn overthrows the Titans and swallows the last remaining goddess who threatens him – Metis, who is pregnant with Athena, subsequently born from Zeus' head. Divine paternity rests on patricide, infanticide, and the subduing of divine maternity, in narratives filled with furious sexuality and abundant gore.

What differentiates the monotheistic Hebrew creation myth from those of its surrounding cultures is a dual absence: the absence of conflict, and the absence of sexuality. The biblical Genesis describes no combat among deities striving for sovereignty, for there is but one divine Being; and the procreation of the universe from a divine body has been replaced by an abstract bodiless creation. Divine fecundity becomes divine fiat. 'The religion of Israel has been conceived as a unique or isolated phenomenon, radically or wholly discontinuous with its environment', as Frank Moore Cross observes, in part because of the apparent distinctiveness of its deity.[11] Yet, as Cross and others demonstrate, the worship of Jahweh was far from uncontested, nor do the Hebrew writings spring forth independently of ancient analogues and antecedents. Rather, biblical literature itself is in origin 'but the continuation of the antecedent Canaanite literature', as Hebrew is an offshoot – a dialect – of Ugaritic. Umberto Cassuto catalogues the numerous verbal formulas including stock epithets, metaphors, and similes, correlated parallelisms, formulas of transition, etc., shared by Canaanite and Hebrew texts.[12] Jahweh absorbs and synthesizes the characteristics of several Canaanite gods, while the struggles between the gods of heaven and the netherworld in Canaanite myth become in Hebrew myth the futile rebellions of creatures against their creator hinted at in occasional 'poetic' biblical passages. Most interestingly for the purposes of feminist analysis, Cassuto and others hypothesize behind Jahweh's conquest of the sea (referred to in the Song of the Sea in Exodus, but also in a variety of passages in Psalms, Isaiah, the Book of Job, and the Apocrypha) a primeval Hebrew myth ascribing to Jahweh the victories ascribed in Canaanite epic to the great goddess Anath in her battle against the netherworld god Mot and his ally, Prince of the Sea.[13]

Unlike Freud, we no longer believe that the murder of the mother goddess was the perfect crime. Both Judaism and Christianity define themselves in absolute opposition to paganism. Yet we know from the prophets' bitter denunciations, as well as from the historic records of Judges, 1 and 2 Samuel, and 1 and 2 Kings, that popular worship of Asherah and Anath remained a recurrent problem in Israel, not eradicated before the fall of the second temple.[14] Patai argues, indeed, that Judaism has never been without some form of goddess in disguise, whether she be figured as Hokhmah, Wisdom, in the Apocrypha, or the Shekhinah in Kabbala, or even the demonic Lilith in Jewish legend and folklore. Similarly, as Elaine Pagels has observed, it was only with difficulty that the early Christian church rooted out as heretical certain images of the Triune God as a trinity of Mother, Father, and Infant; and, as Marina Warner shows in *Alone of All Her Sex*, the figure of Mary – minimally present in the Gospels – develops throughout the history of Christian liturgy, poetry, and iconography in ways that make her seem the Christian avatar of forgotten pagan goddesses. Studies of European witchcraft argue as well for the survival of the 'old religion' of fertility cults in the countryside. In both high culture and folk religion, then, we may witness the seepage of paganism back into the traditions designed to destroy it.

The repressed of biblical narrative is not, in sum, the slain Father but the slain (and immortal) Mother. But, if this is so, the feminist reader, pursuing what Naomi Schor has called 'clitoral hermeneutics', may recover – in those very texts whose object was the erasure of the memory of polytheism – traces of the goddesses who existed in Canaan and throughout the Near East before the advent of monotheism and the victory of the Father. The question then to ask is: what sorts of hints or suggestions of female divinity do we find within or between the lines of patriarchal Scripture? To seek is to encounter an interesting array of possibilities or lines of speculation, some of which are philological, others of which are narrative. The tohu-bohu or formless void of Genesis 1 is related to the Hebrew *tehom*, or void, behind which perhaps stands Tiamat, the goddess destroyed by Marduk. The Eve of Genesis may be related to goddess figures who for millennia throughout the Middle East were associated with gardens, sacred trees, and oracular snakes, whose power over the process of childbirth was appropriated by Jahweh.[15] Her title, 'Mother of all Living', was the title of the goddess Araru whose priestess initiates the savage Enkidu sexually in *Gilgamesh*, thus making him 'wise . . . like a god', as well as teaching him to eat and wear clothing like a man instead of a beast.[16] The late Bronze Age 'Astarte' (or Anath) plaques found throughout Canaan depict the nude goddess grasping lilies, or snakes, or both, in her upraised hands. That the Hebrew Hawwah, Eve, may stem from the same verb for *to be* as does Jahweh, suggests that, at some point prior to Eve's demotion to Adam's mate, Eve and God may have been consorts. The epithet whereby God identifies himself to the patriarchs, El Shaddai, derives from a word which in Hebrew means breast, and in Akkadian means mountain, so that the name plausibly means God of the breast-mountain. Jacob's final blessing of Joseph (Genesis 49: 25–6) invokes Shaddai, 'who shall bless thee with blessings of heaven above, blessings of the deep that lieth under, blessings of the breasts and of the womb . . . unto the utmost bound of the everlasting hills'. Frank Moore Cross associates this passage with the creation account of *Enuma Elish*, in which the breasts of Tiamat become mountains with gushing springs.[17]

But there are subtler traces as well, for which we must look at what Geoffrey Hartman calls 'the unsaid as well as the said, the unmarked as well as the marked terrain'[18] of Scripture, with an ear for oddness in the narrative. Let me invite you now to consider two important biblical

episodes, Genesis 22: 1–18, the *Akedah* or the Binding
of Isaac, which is followed by the episode of the death
and burial of Sarah; and Numbers 20: 1, the death of
Miriam, followed by the episode in which Moses strikes
the rock to obtain water. Both narratives contain puz-
zling and disturbing elements which are resolvable
through the hypothesis that the stories encode acts of
deep historical and cultural repression.

## II

The *Akedah* story (Genesis 22) occupies a central if
occluded position in Judeo-Christian culture from the
middle ages to Kierkegaard and beyond, bearing a
weight of ambivalence and disturbance comparable to
that of the Oedipus story in classical tradition. I quote
it here in its compact entirety:

> And it came to pass after these things that God did
> tempt Abraham, and said unto him, Abraham: and he
> said, Behold, here I am. And he said, Take now thy son,
> thine only son Isaac, whom thou lovest, and get thee
> into the land of Moriah; and offer him there for a burnt
> offering upon one of the mountains which I will tell thee
> of. And Abraham rose up early in the morning, and
> saddled his ass, and took two of his young men with him,
> and Isaac his son, and clave the wood for the burnt
> offering, and rose up, and went unto the place of which
> God had told him. Then on the third day Abraham lifted
> up his eyes and saw the place afar off. And Abraham
> said unto his young men, Abide ye here with the ass;
> and I and the lad will go yonder and worship, and come
> again to you. And Abraham took the wood of the burnt
> offering, and laid it upon Isaac his son; and he took the
> fire in his hand, and a knife; and they went both of them
> together. And Isaac spake unto Abraham his father, and

said, My father: and he said, Here am I, my son. And
he said, Behold the fire and the wood: but where is the
lamb for a burnt offering? And Abraham said, my son,
God will provide himself a lamb for the burnt offering:
so they went both of them together. And they came to
the place which God had told him of; and Abraham built
an altar there, and laid the wood in order, and bound
Isaac his son, and laid him on the altar upon the wood.
And Abraham stretched forth his hand, and took the
knife to slay his son. And the Angel of the Lord called
to him out of heaven, and said, Abraham, Abraham: and
he said, Here am I. And he said, Lay not thine hand
upon the child, neither do thou any thing to him: for
now I know that thou fearest God, seeing that thou hast
not withheld thy son, thine only son, from me. And
Abraham lifted up his eyes, and looked, and behold
behind him a ram caught in a thicket by his horns: and
Abraham went and took the ram, and offered him up for
a burnt offering in the stead of his son.

Normatively read as a narrative exemplifying the virtue
of Abraham's faith and the final confirmation of the
covenant between God and Abraham, the *Akedah* is in
a feminist reading a narrative of gender politics which
inscribes the 'binding' of the sons to the theocentric
world of the fathers. Carol Delaney argues that Abraham
(whose name means 'the father is exalted' and whose
penis is the site and guarantee of the covenant) embodies
the idea that the engendering of children is predominantly a paternal, not maternal, act. Delaney claims that
there exists no evidence of child sacrifice in the time of
Abraham, and therefore the meaning of the *Akedah* 'is
to be found not in the ending of the practice of child
sacrifice but in the establishment of father-right'[19] over
the prior institution of mother-right. I want to argue
that this is a primary meaning of the story, whether or
not it also refers to the substitution of animal for human
sacrifice.

In the story of Abraham before the *Akedah*, the figure of Sarah is already a source of narrative tension, since Abraham has been promised progeny which will be as the sands of the sea and the stars of the sky, yet Sarah is barren. As Mary Callaway and others have shown, the recurrent figure of the barren mother in the Genesis narratives represents the power of the Father-God over fertility, a process formerly female. But there is more to Sarah than a womb. For the same passages of Genesis which concern Sarah's initial barrenness and later fertility represent her also as a commanding personality in her marriage relation. Sarah's offer of Hagar to Abraham is intended to her own advantage, reflecting lawcodes under which barren women were legally entitled to children fathered by their husbands on their servant-women, and were entitled as well to punish such servant-women if they grew impudent, as Hagar does. Sarah's skeptical laughter when she overhears God say that she will have her own son, her later triumphant laugh when that son is circumcized, and the name, Isaac, which memorializes the mother's laughter, emphasize her independent existence and her capacity for pride and pleasure. Sarah's lengthy rivalry with and triumph over Hagar, despite her husband's reluctance, all represent the legitimate wife as a locus of genuine force. Throughout this material the first matriarch is aggressive, wilful, protective of her prerogatives, a lively and formidable personality. Of particular significance in the Abraham–Sarah drama is dialogue, and the consistent pattern of Sarah's assertion and Abraham's obedience:

> And Sarai said unto Abram, Behold now, the Lord hath restrained me from bearing: I pray thee, go in unto my maid; it may be that I shall obtain children by her. And Abram hearkened to the voice of his wife. (Genesis 16: 2)

And Sarai said unto Abram, My wrong be upon thee: I
have given my maid unto thy bosom; and when she saw
that she had conceived, I was despised in her eyes: the
Lord judge between me and thee. But Abram said unto
Sarai, Behold, thy maid is in thy hand; do to her as it
pleaseth thee. (Genesis 16: 5–6)

In the meeting at Mamre, ninety-year-old Sarah eaves-
drops on the conversation between God and Abraham:

Therefore, Sarah laughed within herself, saying, After I
am waxed old shall I have pleasure, my lord being old
also? (Genesis 18: 12)

At Isaac's circumcision Abraham does not speak but
Sarah does, announcing her triumph:

God hath made me to laugh, so that all that hear will
laugh with me. And she said, who would have said unto
Abraham, that Sarah should have given children suck?
for I have born him a son in his old age. (Genesis 21:
6–7)

Sarah's final speech is her command to Abraham at Isaac's
weaning feast, after she sees Hagar's son 'mocking':[20]

Cast out this bondwoman and her son; for the son of
this bondwoman shall not be heir with my son, even with
Isaac. And the thing was very grievous in Abraham's
sight, because of his son. And God said unto Abraham,
Let it not be grievous in thy sight because of the lad,
and because of thy bondwoman; in all that Sarah hath
said unto thee, hearken unto her voice. (Genesis 21:
10–12)

Sarah takes initiative, she has agency, she has speech,
and above all it is quite clear that Isaac is *her* son. Thus
the complete absence of Sarah from the *Akedah* constitutes a loud silence. Where was Sarah when her

husband took away her son – her laughter – to be sacrificed? The narrative in effect simultaneously provokes us to ask, warns us against asking, and provides, albeit in displaced form, the obvious answer. For the very next episode of Genesis recounts the death of Sarah and Abraham's negotiation for a burial place with the men of Hebron. The episode is as long as the *Akedah*, and dramatizes Abraham's sociopolitical skills as much as the *Akedah* dramatizes his utter obedience to God. The main point is presumably to show that Abraham has legitimately bought and paid generously for the cave at Machpelah in which all the patriarchs of Genesis are buried (and which today remains a holy site for both Jews and Muslims). But an odd quirk of dialogue occurs amid the formal courtesies. Whereas the Hittite elders twice offer the patriarch a sepulchre to 'bury thy dead', he twice declares his intention to 'bury my dead *out of my sight*' (King James Version; italics mine). This interesting phrase, usually erased in modern translations,[21] firmly emphasizes Sarah's disappearance. The Hebrew *mi-l'fanai* literally means 'from my face', or 'from before my face', and idiomatically means 'away from my presence'. A common biblical locution, it is also used when the speaker is God, to express or describe a casting off, as when the seed of Israel 'shall cease from being a nation before me' (Jeremiah 31: 36). Thus the narrative of Abraham's succession records a triple triumph of the Father over the Mother. First the power of the womb to generate life is appropriated by the Holy One, then the connective and sustaining power of the umbilical cord becomes the controlling power of the dead rope that binds Isaac, and thirdly Sarah herself must not merely die and be buried but must be eliminated from presence, that is from consciousness. Sarah's burial signals that the defeat of maternal power is the condition/consequence of the male covenant. Medieval midrash, which explains Sarah's death as caused by the *Akedah* (Satan tells her Isaac is dead and she dies of grief, or she learns he is alive and dies of joy),[22] intuitively grasped this point very well.

My second example of a female burial is that of the prophetess Miriam, near the close of the Exodus narrative. Here again, we are looking at traces of a woman's story embedded in a larger narrative which is overwhelmingly masculine, and now on a larger scale. Genesis is the story of the covenant between God and Abraham, extended to Abraham's progeny. It is, in effect, the saga of a single nomadic family. The thrust of the Exodus account and the wanderings in the wilderness is to reinscribe the covenant between God and his chosen people as national rather than biological. At this point, both God and his chosen ones enter history. From a feminist perspective, however, the Exodus narrative might be read as a second Fall of Man in which the values of the family – peace, prosperity, progeny, and a lively relationship between husbands and wives – are gradually replaced by the values of nationhood, which are military, priestly, and legal.

In the early portion of the story the prophetess Miriam is one of a set of powerful transgressive females (the midwives, Jochabed, Miriam, the daughter of Pharaoh, and later Zipporah) who may be seen as colluding across ethnic and class boundaries and against patriarchal power to preserve the life of the hero, Moses. The midwives lie to Pharaoh to avoid killing Hebrew firstborns; Jochabed sets her infant son in a basket on the Nile; Pharaoh's daughter adopts him; his sister Miriam suggests Jochabed as the wetnurse (Exodus 1: 15 to 2: 10). All this material has very much the air of folktale, which might well mean that women had a voice in its composition. Later in the narrative the Midianite wife of Moses, Zipporah, saves Moses from a nocturnal attack by God, in a cryptic episode to which I will refer below (Exodus 4: 24–6). When the Israelites cross the Red Sea,

Miriam leads the Israelite women in song and dance. Significantly, although the children of Israel have left Egypt in haste, carrying only necessities, the women have their musical instruments, their timbrels; this suggests the ritual importance of women at this stage of the Exodus, as does the fact that Miriam is here called 'the prophetess' (Exodus 15: 20–1). By the end of the Exodus story, however, Miriam embodies the humiliation and defeat of female influence. Other women have by now disappeared from the narrative:

> And Miriam and Aaron spake against Moses because of the Ethiopian woman whom he had married: for he had married an Ethiopian woman. And they said, hath the Lord indeed spoken only by Moses? hath he not spoken also by us? And the Lord heard it. . . . And the Lord spake suddenly unto Moses, and unto Aaron, and unto Miriam, Come out ye three unto the tabernacle of the congregation. And they three came out. And the Lord came down in the pillar of the cloud, and stood in the door of the tabernacle, and called Miriam and Aaron: and they both came forth. And he said, Hear now my words: If there be a prophet among you, I the Lord will make myself known to him in a vision, and will speak to him in a dream. My servant Moses is not so. . . . With him will I speak mouth to mouth, even apparently, and not in dark speeches; and the similitude of the Lord shall he behold: wherefore then were ye not afraid to speak against my servant Moses? And the anger of the Lord was kindled against them; and he departed. And the cloud departed from off the tabernacle; and behold, Miriam became leprous, white as snow: and Aaron looked upon Miriam, and behold, she was leprous. (Numbers 12: 1–10)

Moses begs God to heal Miriam, but 'the Lord said unto Moses, If her father had but spit in her face, should she not be ashamed seven days? let her be shut out from the camp seven days, and after that let her be received in again. And Miriam was shut out from the camp seven days, and the people journeyed not till Miriam was brought in again' (Numbers 12: 14–15). Thus Aaron and Miriam together challenge the authority of Moses; Miriam alone is punished with leprosy and ostracism. Miriam's subsequent death in the narrative is almost unmarked, whereas Aaron's is followed by elaborate mourning.

The episode immediately after Miriam's death is a drought. Here is the passage: 'Then came the children of Israel, even the whole congregation, into the desert of Zin in the first month: and the people abode in Kadesh; and Miriam died there, and was buried there. And there was no water for the congregation: and they gathered themselves together against Moses and against Aaron' (Numbers 20: 1–2). At first this seems to be just another in the endless series of Israelite backslidings or murmurings against the authority of Moses, a rebellion to which Moses responds by striking the rock to which God has led him, to produce water. The perplexing element now is that God construes Moses' action as a sin, for which he is punished by being forbidden to enter the Promised Land.

Why so severe a penalty for what seems a misdemeanor, the striking of a rock to produce water instead of talking to the rock? We may conclude that Jahweh at this point is being more than usually arbitrary, or we may try to invent a moral reason as mainstream rabbinical interpretation does. We may also posit a repressed tradition in which Miriam is a far more significant figure than she appears to be in the biblical text; we may even wonder whether it is somehow Miriam who is violated when the rock is struck. Two minor points within the text offer clues to the possibility of such a tradition. One is that Aaron seems to have been a late addition to a story in which Miriam alone challenges Moses, for the verb of complaint is in the feminine singular. Then, the complaint about Moses' Ethiopian wife is a mysterious one since this wife is mentioned nowhere else. According to one kabbalistic interpretation, Moses' 'Black Bride' symbolizes the written laws and stone commandments – the 'black fire' of the written law as against the 'white fire' of the unwritten. Thus Miriam's challenge might suggest that she herself represents the unwritten, hermetic Torah of mystical yearning.

But what is Miriam's connection with the drought? Let us recall that Miriam has previously been associated with water in the narrative, at the birth of Moses and at the crossing of the Red Sea; that her name means 'bitter sea' or 'water'; that the place where water is found, Meribah, as Devorah Steinmetz points out, 'means contentiousness and is linked in the episode which immediately follows Miriam's death with the word MRY, rebelliousness' (Numbers 20: 10, 24; 27: 14), and parallels an earlier drought-episode punning on Miriam's name, that of Marah (Exodus 15: 20–5).[23] Here again, as with Sarah's death, rabbinical commentary insists on the connection which the biblical text only implies. For the midrashic tradition develops in elaborate form the legend of Miriam's well. In some versions it was a well wrought by God on the second day of creation to honor the future merits of Miriam, and to have been discovered in turn by each of the patriarchs and matriarchs in the desert. It is supposed to have followed the wanderings of the Israelites in the desert, pausing always opposite the tabernacle, and to have disappeared at her death. The same well is successfully invoked in Numbers 21: 17 at Be-er, 'Then Israel sang this song, Spring up, O well; sing ye unto it',[24] perhaps recalling the song of Miriam at the Red Sea or her leadership of singing women.

Near Eastern myths and rituals often involve goddesses who resurrect dying gods emblematic of the cycles of agrarian fertility. Ilana Pardes speculates that there is a goddess, possibly Isis, 'behind' all the women of the Exodus narrative.[25] My reading of Miriam would dovetail with the way Pardes reads Zipporah's rescue of Moses ('a bloody husband thou art to me') as an Isis who preserves the life of her consort Osiris. It would also want to recall the specifically Canaanite variant in which Anath defeats the powers of water – 'I smote El's beloved, Sea, / I destroyed the great rivers of El' – and resurrects her own beloved brother Baal, and would want to remember that one of the epithets of the high goddess Asherah, with whom Anath was at times conflated, was 'Asherah of the Sea'. Does the biblical Miriam, then, represent all that remains of a formerly great goddess or goddesses who exercised control over the terrestrial waters? We can do no more than speculate upon this possibility, but we can also do no less.[26]

## III

The Sarah and Miriam stories are of course not the only biblical episodes conforming to the pattern I have described, in which women are foregrounded as active agents at the beginning of a story, and disappear by the end of it. Rebecca, the wife of Isaac, 'went to inquire of the Lord' regarding the two children who struggled in her womb,

> And the Lord said unto her, Two nations are in thy womb, and two manner of people shall be separated from thy bowels; and the one people shall be stronger than the other people; and the elder shall serve the younger. (Genesis 25: 23)

Rebecca ensures by trickery that her favored son Jacob receives Isaac's blessing and that he will marry matri-locally. She then disappears from the narrative, not to return. Following the romantic love of Jacob for Rachel, the intensely comic sexual rivalry between Rachel and Leah, and Rachel's bold theft of Laban's household gods, both Rachel and Leah vanish from the narrative after the birth of the final son, Benjamin, although it is only Rachel who dies in childbirth (Genesis 35: 16–20). Judah's widowed daughter-in-law Tamar disguises herself as a harlot in order to obtain justice, and progeny, from Judah, who has refused to wed her to his remaining son in accordance with custom. She thereby ensures the survival of that one of the twelve tribes from which the Davidic monarchy will spring; after this episode, she disappears (Genesis 38). Potiphar's wife in the Joseph cycle disappears after constituting the temptation to Joseph's purity and the device whereby he is thrown into the prison whence he will rise to power (Genesis 39: 7–23). In the Book of Judges, the future birth of Samson and his role as 'a Nazarite unto God from the womb' is revealed not to his father but to his mother, and not once but twice; Manoah in his encounters with the angel steadily misunderstands the message his wife receives (Judges 13: 2–23). But the mother of Samson, and indeed all the females up to and including Delilah in the Samson story, can be read as figures inscribing male desire/dread of the enclosing womb which is mentioned so conspicuously in his nativity narrative and is replicated in the chambers of the inappropriate women he keeps marrying, the repeated 'bindings' and 'compassings' he suffers. As Mieke Bal in *Lethal Love* points out, even the architecture of the Samson story is female, down to the 'two middle pillars' of the Philistine temple between which the hero stands as he enacts his *Liebestod*. Samson is the great male escape artist of the Bible. He is also the sacrificial figure who confirms in the flesh, as Isaac so narrowly does not, that the body of the son belongs not to the mother but to a male community and its male God. At Samson's death, the mother who figures so prominently at his birth is absent; instead, 'his brethren and all the

house of his father came down, and took him, and
brought him up, and buried him . . . in the buryingplace
of Manoah his father' (Judges 16: 31). Two further influential females are Hannah, the mother of the prophet
Samuel, and Bathsheba, the mother of Solomon. Both
are instrumental in securing rule for their sons, and both
cease to exist in the narrative when this has been accom-
plished (1 Samuel 1 to 2: 11; 1 Kings 1: 11 to 2: 25).

These female figures are by no means simple parallels
of each other. In some cases they are allies, vessels,
confidantes of Jahweh; in other cases they are enemies.
Some are tricksters, others are not. Most are maternal,
but not all. What they do have in common is what
William Blake centuries later called, with horror, 'female
Will'. In all of these stories the woman represents
Desire. And in each story the disappearance of the
female coordinates or coincides with the establishment
(or reestablishment following a rebellion or fall) of the
exclusively male covenant.

So far as I am aware, no biblical critic has noticed this
startlingly recurrent pattern in biblical narrative. I assume this is because everyone *takes it for granted* that
women must be rejected in order for the story of male
maturity, male leadership, male heroism, to take place.
The pattern has promulgated itself so successfully that
it has become invisible. But I submit that what feminist
hermeneutics finds at the textual fault-lines of such
stories is the obsessively told and re-told moment of
transition from a world in which women were humanly
and socially powerful because divinity was in part female,
to a world in which that divinity and power were repressed. I submit, in my revision of Freud's formulation,
that the imperfectly repressed memory of the Great
Mother's murder is among the most profound sources
of energy within Judaism, and perhaps Christianity as
well, as the work of Elaine Pagels and Marina Warner
would suggest. I submit that the biblical narrator whom

we are tempted to consider the uniquely *un*belated author in our culture is precisely the opposite: the original exemplar of literary belatedness. How well we know that voice, whose tremendous verbal sublimity becomes at its most sublime the voice of a male God who demands over and over, across the texts and across the centuries, that we have no other Gods but Him, and has been able to make that command stick, more or less, for at least two thousand years. It is a voice – listen to it – which depends utterly on the need to deny that there were ever any previous texts, previous powers in the universe. 'I thy God am a jealous God.' We recognize it all too well. But who is this God so anxious about his dominance that he requires absolute obedience like any petty human tyrant? And why does it never occur to us that a genuinely omnipotent being might *not* require worship, might *not* demand obedience, might *not* have any reason to inspire fear in the objects of its love?

Is it possible that the whole story of canonicity, the whole story of authority in our culture, is intimately bound up with the repressed Mother, shimmering and struggling at the liminal threshold of consciousness, against whom the Father must anxiously defend himself? So it appears to me. It remains to be seen whether a return of the repressed will be equally possible – whether, as feminist theology and the women's spirituality movement in America propose, a rebirth of the divine female may be occurring in our time. That is the ultimate theme of my second lecture, which looks at how women poets (re)read and (re)write the Bible.

NOTES

1   Edmund Jabès, *Adam, or the Birth of Anxiety*, tr. of *Le Livre du Partage* (Paris: Gallimard, 1987) by Rosemarie

Waldrop, *Tel Aviv Review* 2 (Fall 1989/ Winter 1990), p. 11.

2   Hélène Cixous and Catherine Clément, *The Newly Born Woman* (originally *La Jeune Née*), tr. Betsy Wing, Introduction by Sandra M. Gilbert (Minneapolis: University of Minnesota Press, 1986), p. 6.

3   Mieke Bal, *Lethal Love: Feminist Literary Readings of Biblical Love Stories* (Bloomington: Indiana University Press, 1987), p. 132.

4   Alicia Ostriker, *Stealing the Language: The Emergence of Women's Poetry in America* (Boston: Beacon Press, 1986), pp. 11, 210–38.

5   Adrienne Rich, 'When We Dead Awaken: Writing as Re-vision', in *On Lies, Secrets, and Silence: Selected Prose 1966–1978* (New York: W. W. Norton, 1979), p. 35.

6   Sigmund Freud, *Moses and Monotheism*, tr. Katherine Jones (New York: Vintage, 1939), pp. 52, 121. Compare Fredric Jameson's conviction that what is repressed in texts is the narrative of class struggle which a Marxist hermeneutic can recover: 'It is in detecting the traces of that uninterrupted narrative, in restoring to the surface of the text the repressed and buried reality of this fundamental history, that the doctrine of a political unconscious finds its function and its necessity': *The Political Unconscious: Narrative as a Socially Symbolic Act* (Ithaca: Cornell University Press, 1981), p. 20. Jonathan Culler's assumption that the 'unconscious' of a text is accessible through 'linguistic traces and effects' and Riffaterre's similar notion of a 'verbal unconscious' buried inside the manifest words of a text are variations on this theme. Jameson quotes *The Communist Manifesto*: 'The history of all hitherto existing society is the history of class struggles: freeman and slave, patrician and plebeian, lord and serf, guild-master and journeyman – in a word, oppressor and oppressed – stood in constant opposition to one another, and carried on an uninterrupted, now hidden, now open fight, a fight that each time ended, either in a revolutionary reconstitution of society at large, or in the common ruin of the contending classes': Karl Marx, *On Revolution*, ed. and tr. S. K. Padover (New York: McGraw-Hill,

1971), p. 81. To such a list of class opponents, a feminist
naturally adds men and women, and therefore is ready to
assume that woman's struggle with man is repressed in
texts, yet can be restored to their surfaces. The more
sacred the text, one might add, the more significant both
the repression and the potential restoration.

7   *Moses and Monotheism*, p. 144.

8   Raphael Patai, *The Hebrew Goddess* (New York: Avon,
1978), pp. 15–16.

9   Gerda Lerner, *The Creation of Patriarchy* (New York:
Oxford University Press, 1986), p. 145.

10  John A. Phillips, *Eve: The History of an Idea* (San Francisco:
Harper & Row, 1984), p. 4.

11  Frank Moore Cross, *Canaanite Myth and Hebrew Epic*
(Cambridge, Mass.: Harvard University Press, 1973), p. viii.

12  Umberto Cassuto, *The Goddess Anath: Canaanite Epics of
the Patriarchal Age*, tr. Israel Abrahams (Jerusalem: Mag-
nes Press, 1971), pp. 17–20.

13  Cassuto, pp. 71–3. Anath, daughter of El and sister of
Baal, is both a warrior and a fertility goddess whose cult
spread from Canaan to Egypt in the eighteenth and nineteenth dynasties; in a temple built in the time of Rameses
II (thirteenth century BC), a pillar is dedicated to Anath
queen of heaven and mistress of all the gods. Temples
were dedicated to her in Canaan, whence we have place
names like Beth-anath (house of Anath) in Joshua 19: 38
and Judges 1: 33 and Beth-anoth (Joshua 15: 59). Cross
massively confirms the continuity of ancient Hebrew with
ancient Canaanite culture, arguing that the Mosaic covenant was grafted onto a tribal religion of the fathers. The
Canaanite god El is portrayed as father and creator, not
as a nature deity; like Jahweh he is a warrior; his abode
is in some texts a tent, in some a palace, sometimes 'in
the far north' at the 'mountain of El'; the descriptions fit
'Eden the garden of God at the mount of God' in Ezekiel.
His epithets, 'god of the covenant', 'El the judge', 'eternal king', etc., carry over to Jahweh, whose name Cross
speculates might derive from the Canaanite/Proto-
Hebrew verb 'to be'. The description of the tabernacle,
its curtains embroidered with cherubim, and its cherubim

throne, its proportions modelled on the cosmic shrine,
'all reflect Canaanite modes, and specifically the Tent of
El and his cherubim throne' (Cross, p. 72). John Day, in
*God's Conflict with the Dragon of the Sea: Echoes of a
Canaanite Myth in the Old Testament* (Cambridge: Cambridge University Press, 1985), confirms that 'the Old
Testament's use of the imagery of the divine conflict with
the dragon and the sea is appropriated from Canaanite
mythology, deriving from the myth of Baal's conflict with
the sea-god Yam and his dragon associate Leviathan . . .
and not from the Babylonian myth of Marduk's conflict
with Tiamat recounted in Enuma Elish' (p. 179). The
imagery was used in celebrations of the autumn festival
and associated with Jahweh's enthronement as king (parallel to Baal's enthronement), Day speculates, before it
became demythologized.

14  See Merlin Stone, *When God Was a Woman* (New York:
Harcourt Brace, 1976), and Raphael Patai, *The Hebrew
Goddess*, as suggestive and speculative works, and Gerda
Lerner, *The Creation of Patriarchy*, as definitively historical. 'The persistence of popular goddess worship in regions
where male gods officially dominated is widely documented:
The Great Goddess may have been demoted in the pantheon of the gods, but she continued to be worshipped.
. . . All Assyriologists testify to her enormous popularity
and the persistence of her cult, in various guises, in all
the major cities of the Near East for nearly two thousand
years. . . . Statuaries in her likeness and with her symbols
are widespread, testifying to her popularity . . . found not
only in temples but in homes, indicating the important
place of her worship in popular religion': Lerner, pp. 158–9.

15  Lerner, chs 7 and 9.

16  E. A. Speiser (tr.), 'The Epic of Gilgamesh: Akkadian
Myths and Epics', in *Ancient Near Eastern Texts Relat-
ing to the Old Testament*, ed. James Pritchard (Princeton:
Princeton University Press, 1955), p. 75.

17  Cross, pp. 55–6.

18  Geoffrey Hartman, 'The Struggle for the Text', in *Midrash and Literature*, eds Geoffrey Hartman and Sanford
Budick (New Haven: Yale University Press, 1986), p. 3.

19   Carol Delaney, 'The Legacy of Abraham', in *Beyond Androcentrism: New Essays on Women and Religion*, ed. Rita Gross (Missoula, Mont.: Scholars Press, 1977), p. 230. Frank Moore Cross, however, claims that child sacrifice was part of the cult of the Canaanite El, and that 'an echo of this aspect of the El cult is probably heard in the biblical tradition that the first-born belonged to the deity, and in the background of Isaac's sacrifice' (p. 26).

20   'Mocking' is King James Version; other translations give 'playing'; there may be a sexual connotation to the term used.

21   'Out of my sight' is in the King James Version and the Jewish Publication Society Bibles. This embarrassing sense is erased in translations which speak of 'a proper burial' or of 'removing the body for burial'.

22   Louis Ginsberg, *The Legends of the Jews*, vol. 1 (Philadelphia: Jewish Publication Society, 1933), pp. 286–7.

23   Devorah Steinmetz, 'A Portrait of Miriam in Rabbinic Midrash', *Prooftexts* 8, no. 1 (January 1988), p. 55.

24   'God wrought this great miracle for the merits of the prophetess Miriam, wherefore also it was called "Miriam's well". But this well dates back to the beginning of the world, for God created it on the second day of the creation': Ginsberg, pp. 126–7. It was the same well over which Abraham's and Abimelech's men contended, it followed the Israelites in the wilderness and always settled opposite the tabernacle; the leaders of the twelve tribes with their staffs would chant to it and make it gush forth as high as pillars (pp. 50–4). The well vanished at Miriam's death (p. 318). Penina V. Adelman, *Miriam's Well* (Fresh Meadows, NY: Biblio Press, 1986), p. 64, mentions the claim of the Kaballists of Safed to have rediscovered Miriam's well near the Sea of Galilee and the custom of filling pouches with its water to carry to Jewish settlements throughout the diaspora, as well as the later Hasidic belief that the well would reappear whenever Jews sang to it, and the still later saying that all wells are filled with waters from Miriam's well at the close of Sabbath, for whoever dips into them at that time. Whoever drinks

from Miriam's well, it is said, gains a purer understanding of Torah.

25   Ilana Pardes, 'Zipporah and the Struggle for Deliverance', *The Shulamite's Song, and Other Counter-Traditions in the Bible* (Cambridge, Mass.: Harvard University Press, forthcoming). Pardes concludes: 'Although Freud failed to perceive the traces left by the Egyptian mother goddess in Exodus (in fact this is the one perfect murder he attributes to Judaism) his analysis of the dynamics of repression is most appropriate. The Egyptian divine protectress is "wrenched apart" as her role is split among the midwives, Yocheved, Miriam, Pharaoh's daughter, and Zipporah. In Zipporah's case she is even displaced to Midian, but with a little bit of detective work her wings may be set into motion once again.'

26   Robert Graves, whose work on goddess religions is turning out to be considerably less harebrained than was formerly thought, refers to the 'Goddess known to the Chaldeans as Marratu, to the Jews as Marah, to the Persians as Mariham, to the Christians as Mary: as well as Marian, Miriam, Mariamne, Myrrhine, Myrtea, Myrrha, Maria and Marina', whose 'blue robe and pearl necklace were classic symbols of the sea, edged with pearly foam'. See Barbara Walker, *The Women's Encyclopedia of Myths and Secrets* (San Francisco: Harper & Row, 1983), p. 584; Robert Graves, *The White Goddess* (London: Faber & Faber, 1948), p. 438. *Mer* was an Egyptian word for both 'waters' and 'mother-love': E. A. Budge, *Egyptian Language* (London: Routledge & Kegan Paul, 1966), p. 76.

# A Word Made Flesh: The Bible and Women's Poetry

*It is a violence within that protects us from a violence with-
out. It is the imagination pressing back against the pressure
of reality. It seems, in the last analysis, to have something to
do with our self-preservation; and that, no doubt, is why the
expression of it, the sound of its words, helps us live our lives.*

Wallace Stevens[1]

she carries a book but it is not
the tome of the ancient wisdom,

the pages, I imagine, are the blank pages
of the unwritten volume of the new.

H. D.[2]

In my first lecture I looked at certain biblical texts as
exemplifying the process whereby patriarchy constitutes
itself: a process in which female power is erased, but
always imperfectly erased so that the erasure has to be
obsessively repeated and is never quite finished. By
necessity my stance as a feminist toward these texts was
adversarial. My object was to retrieve from a patriarchal
narrative what the narrative was trying to destroy. In this
second lecture, however, I cease to posit a simple polarity or adversarial relationship between male text and

female re/writers. Instead, I want to take up that thread
of my argument which claims that what may seem outrageous, blasphemous, and irreligious about woman's
re-imaginings of the Bible is both forbidden and invited
by the very text and tradition she is challenging.

In this lecture I will first survey, briefly, those elements
within the Hebrew Bible and the New Testament which
most clearly encourage transgressive and subversive at-
titudes toward sacred authority, including the authority
of scripture itself. Then I will look at the biblical appropriations of several English and American women poets,
first Emily Dickinson, Elizabeth Barrett Browning and
Christina Rossetti in the nineteenth century, then H. D.
as representing high modernism, and finally the work of
contemporary American women poets. I suggest that
biblical revisionism takes three sometimes overlapping
forms: a hermeneutics of suspicion, a hermeneutics of
desire, and a hermeneutics of indeterminacy. Although
I will not press this point, it seems to me that the ways
women writers deal with biblical texts are paradigmatic
for the ways we deal with male texts and traditions in
general. Indeed, this triple model of (re)interpretive
modes might well serve to describe how writers of any
marginalized group come ultimately to deal with a dominant culture which both inspires and repels them. I would
encourage my readers to consider whether they find this
to be the case.


I


The questioning of authority, including divine authority,
has been built into Judaism in several different ways.
From the moment God confides to Abraham his intention to destroy Sodom and Gomorrah, and Abraham is
appalled and replies, 'Shall the Judge of all the earth not

do justly'? – making clear that he, Abraham, thinks God
has no right to harm innocent people – the right and
even the duty of God's children to interrogate their
father becomes a recurrent biblical theme. 'That be far
from thee', cries Abraham, 'to do after this manner, to
slay the righteous with the wicked: and that the righteous
should be as the wicked.'

> And the Lord said, If I find in Sodom fifty righteous
> within the city, then I will spare all the place for their
> sakes. And Abraham answered and said, behold now, I
> have taken upon me to speak unto the Lord, which am
> but dust and ashes: Peradventure there shall lack five of
> the fifty righteous: wilt thou destroy all the city for the
> lack of five? And he said, if I find there forty and five, I
> will not destroy it. And he spake unto him yet again, and
> said, Peradventure there shall be forty found there.
> (Genesis 18: 25–9)

And so on, until Abraham bargains God down to ten.
In this rather comedic scene we see the origins of Jewish
*chutzpah*. Jacob's wrestling with the angel and Job's challenge to God are similar episodes in different tones: one
heroic, one lyric or rhapsodic. But these are hardly
unique episodes within Judaism. 'Wherefore doth the
way of the wicked prosper?' asks Jeremiah, inaugurating
the tradition of interrogating God's goodness which still
reverberates in contemporary Jewish writers. In Elie
Wiesel's *The Gates of the Forest*, a rabbi in a concentration camp announces to his fellows, 'I intend to convict
God of murder, for he is destroying his people and the
Law he gave them from Mount Sinai. I have irrefutable
proof in my hands.' In I. B. Singer's autobiographical *In
My Father's Court*, the boy Isaac asks himself, 'What did
the Emperor of everything, the Creator of heaven and
Earth require? That he could go on watching soldiers fall
on battlefields?' In Malamud's *The Fixer* occurs this
dialogue: ' "Yakov," said Shmuel passionately, "Don't

forget your God." "Who forgets who?" the fixer said angrily. "What do I get from him but a bang on the head and a stream of piss in my face?" ' Thus the woman poet who challenges what Sylvia Plath calls 'Herr God, Herr Lucifer' continues a tradition of challenge and interrogation of divinity which has been a core theme within Jewish writing.

As to earthly authority: here too the scriptural tradition supports its questioners. The Jews as a nation originate in a slave rebellion; the Exodus story continues to resound in the aspirations and rhetoric of oppressed populations throughout the world, as Michael Walzer observes in *Exodus and Revolution*;[3] the story has inspired generations of African-Americans, from spirituals such as 'Let My People Go' to Martin Luther King's 'I've been to the mountain', in which the soon-to-be-assassinated leader identifies himself with the aged Moses. The role of the prophets includes a steady attack on the Israelite ruling classes, kings and priests alike. Notwithstanding the centrality of ritual in the Israelite community, Isaiah, for example, is the mouthpiece of a God who says, 'Your new moons and your appointed feasts my soul hateth' (Isaiah 1: 14), and demands that his people feed the hungry, clothe the naked, and help the oppressed. 'I hate, I despise your feasts,' cries the God of Amos, 'but let justice roll down like waters' (Amos 5: 21–4). Social justice, as opposed to whatever authority resists it, becomes a core motivation throughout Jewish history, in ways obviously resonant with the consciousness of feminism, as numerous feminist theologians have noted. Rosemary Ruether argues that 'the prophetic-messianic tradition' in which God speaks 'as critic, rather than sanctifier, of the status quo' implies 'a rejection of every elevation of one social group against others as image and agent of God, every use of God to justify social domination and subjugation'.[4]

Like Judaism, Christianity has been from its inception a self-revising tradition, in which the letter of the law killeth while the spirit giveth life, the letter signifying a fixed canon and a privileged set of clerics and theologians to interpret it, while the spirit represents the unmediated truth directly available to the believer. From Christ's repeated defiance of religious law and his mockery of Pharisees and Sadducees, from his announcement that he is himself the fulfillment of Law and its virtual anti-dote, from the powerful conception of social reversal which structures the Sermon on the Mount, from Christ's promise to provide the faithful with the interior guidance of the Holy Spirit, and above all from his insistence that the kingdom of heaven is within us, Christianity throughout its history has produced wave after wave of anti-institutional reform. As often as a church has strengthened its absolute hold over its com-munity, just so often have dissenters guided by one or another version of inner light challenged both dogma and power – appealing always to the high tribunal of the scriptural text itself. The history of Christianity is a history of periodic schisms which are ultimately reinter-pretations of the meaning of the New Testament. Nor is feminist rebellion against fathers, husbands, and polit-ical authorities on Christian grounds confined to the twentieth century. Rather, it is a key theme in Christian martyrology, in the lives of the female saints, in women's conversion narratives. Indeed, wherever women's spiritu-ality has arisen as an independent force, there we are typically reminded that we are to call no man father, master, or lord, and that 'whosoever shall exalt himself shall be abased; and he that humbleth himself shall be exalted' (Matthew 23: 1–12).[5]

Regarding textual canonicity and authority, modern biblical scholarship informs us that the notion of Scrip-ture as a unitary Word dictated or directly inspired by God, a Word presumed to be One like its author, and therefore fixed, changeless, and eternal, has always been a myth. The Hebrew Bible was compiled over a thousand-year period, comparable to the period from Beowulf to T. S. Eliot. Its editing, redaction, and canonization process spans a time from that of Ezra to the composition of the Mishnah, from about 400 BC to AD 200. Some of its written sources go back as far as the third millennium BC and include Sumerian, Babylonian, Egyptian, and Canaanite myth and poetry, while the wisdom literature such as Proverbs and Job comes very late and is strongly Hellenistic. Of the New Testament, no portion was written during the lifetime of Christ; the synoptic Gospels offer inconsistent versions of numerous stories; a consensus exists among scholars that four of the fourteen Pauline epistles are pseudonymous and that another three may be so. Although most Christians identify John of Patmos, author of Revelation, with John the beloved disciple of Christ, most scholars today agree that he was probably an itinerant Christian prophet writing in Asia Minor in the final decade of the first century. The establishment of a fixed canon, excluding as heretical numerous gospels, epistles, narratives, and prophecies which formed part of early Christian literature, took place between the second and fourth centuries AD. Elaine Pagels makes clear that the stigma of heresy in the developing Christian church fell on texts that denied the need for a priesthood to mediate the relationship between humanity and divinity, and/or on texts that represented divinity as partially female.[6]

To historicize the Bible is to recognize that sacred writ is intrinsically no more absolute in its authority than other writing. For its authority is always socially constituted, yet always attempts to represent itself as divine. 'Not least of the elements that enter into the very nature of religion', one biblical scholar observes, 'is the necessity that lies upon it ... to change while both seeming changeless and protesting its changelessness.'[7]

It is essential for the feminist critic to remember that Scripture has at no single moment in its history been a unified, monolithic text, has always been a radically layered, plurally authored, multiply motivated composite, full of fascinating mysteries, gaps, and inconsistencies, a garden of delight to the exegete. Contemporary critics find in Scripture a kind of paradise of polysemy. 'The really significant elements in biblical narrative are the contradictions', claim the structuralists Leach and Aycock.[8] Roland Barthes remarks: 'What interests me most . . . is . . . the abrasive frictions, the breaks, the discontinuities of readability, the juxtaposition of narrative entities which to some extent run free from an explicit logical articulation.'[9] Geoffrey Hartman enjoys 'the fault lines of a text, the evidence of a narrative sediment that has not entirely settled', and proposes that biblical writing is 'a fusion of heterogeneous stories . . . layered' like Lévi-Strauss's *bricolage* in myth, or Bakhtin's heteroglossia in novels.[10] Robert Alter stresses the contradictions and debates within biblical texts as well as their unities.[11] But the reader for whom the text is genuinely sacred may be at least as engaged with its radical indeterminacies as the secular critic:

> For what is at issue with respect to the Scriptures is not what lies behind the text in the form of an (always elusive) original meaning but what lies in front of it where the interpreter stands. The Bible always addresses itself to the time of interpretation. . . . If the text does not apply to us it is an empty text. . . . We take the text in relation to ourselves, understanding ourselves in its light, even as our situation throws *its* light upon the text, allowing it to disclose itself differently, perhaps in unheard-of ways.[12]

Within the very temple of fixity, then, lives the invisible daimon of flux: 'Revelation is not something that occurs once for all and is now over and done with.'[13]

## II

In her second letter to Thomas Wentworth Higginson, written in April 1862, Emily Dickinson describes her family: 'They are religious, except me, and address an eclipse, every morning, whom they call their Father.' Dickinson here is testing the waters of Higginson's tolerance for verbal mischief. As a critique of conventional religiousness she may mean that Christians routinely lack any real notion of God; or that the God they worship remains (deliberately?) remote, invisible to them; or that they are actually worshipping their own shadows; or that there is no God. In her poems Dickinson is no less bold, no less impudent. 'The Bible is an antique Volume / Written by faded Men',[14] which as a woman she feels quite free to criticize, to mock, to rewrite, and to use for her own purposes.

One purpose is critique: the God Dickinson has been taught to propitiate is, in her judgement, manipulative, brutal, and indifferent to human suffering. 'Of course – I prayed – / And did God care?' (376). Omnipotence extorts worship in a divinely monopolistic economy where we are beggars and he is the 'Burglar! Banker – Father' (49), the 'mighty Merchant' (621) who meanly withholds his goods from the would-be purchaser. He is 'Inquisitor', 'mastiff', a 'God of flint'. Can we know if he is real? His inaccessibility – 'I know that He exists / Somewhere – in Silence' – is perhaps but 'an instant's play' designed to make immortality a more blissful surprise. But, then again, perhaps not: 'Should the play / Prove piercing earnest', the joke would have 'crawled too far' (338). Dickinson's portrait of the biblical bully who

> On Moses seemed to fasten
> With tantalizing play

As Boy should deal with lesser Boy
To prove Ability

(597)

leads her again to an epistemological paradox. Although she readily acknowledges that the story is fiction, 'in soberer moments / No Moses can there be', the cruelty of this 'Romance' continues to torment her:

Old Man on Nebo – late as this –
My justice bleeds – for Thee!

Whatever awe Emily Dickinson experiences for the God of her Fathers is more than balanced by rage at his power and distance, not to mention fury at his possible nonexistence. Yet anyone who reads Dickinson at all recognizes that her poetry is saturated with biblical allusions which represent desire at its most intense, blissful, and playful. Fantasies of heaven and paradise stream through her work, not merely as a figure for the transcendent and unattainable (' "Heaven" is what I cannot reach'; 239), but precisely as a figure for earthly and immanent joy. Staying home from church to hear the birds preach, Emily finds that instead of getting to heaven later, she's going all the time. Inebriate of air and debauchee of dew, she imagines herself admired by the saints and angels as the 'little Tippler / Leaning against the Sun', presumably replacing the woman clothed with the sun of Revelation. The palpable eroticism of 'Come slowly – Eden –' and the thoroughly orgasmic and possibly lesbian fantasy of 'Rowing in Eden – / Ah, the Sea!' in 'Wild Nights – Wild Nights!' make paradise regained a locus of gratified sexuality. Pursuing her erotic dramas, Dickinson is 'Empress of Calvary' (1072) and usurps a lover's crucifix (1736) in an exhibitionistic demonstration of her own superior pain. She archly questions Paul's condemnation of the flesh as 'sown in dishonour'

by her own reading of both Bible and body: 'Not so
fast! / Apostle is askew' (62). She likes, unsurprisingly,
the story of Jacob, who 'Found he had worsted God!'
She identifies at times with the Satan who walks to and
fro on the earth, at times with the Eve whose burial place
is unknown ('and why am I not Eve?'). She feminizes
God as a mother bird who notices when her sparrows
fall (164) and as the Typic Mother in whose Book June
and Autumn are Genesis and Revelation (1115). She
incarnates and eroticizes language itself in 'A Word
made Flesh' (1651), a poem which crosses the boundaries dividing spirit and flesh, the transcendent and the
immanent:

> A Word made Flesh is seldom
> And tremblingly partook
> Nor then perhaps reported
> But have I not mistook
> Each one of us has tasted
> With ecstasies of stealth
> the very food debated
> To our specific strength –
> A Word that breathes distinctly
> Has not the power to die
> Cohesive as the Spirit
> It may expire if He –
> 'Made Flesh and dwelt among us'
> Could condescension be
> Like this consent of Language
> This loved Philology.

Let me suggest just a few of the outrageous ideas which
seem incorporated here. First, the incarnate Christ who
in this poem is eaten with ecstasies of stealth (spiritual
ecstasy being indivisible from sensual) is distinguished
from the publicly consumed Christ of the churches, and
may even be distinguished from the publicly 'reported'
Christ of Scripture. He is dangerous; he is also multiple,

a food that varies with the eater. In the poem's second half he becomes, moreover, fused with, or infused into, a poetic Word whose immortality consists paradoxically in the fleshly embodying which makes it a 'loved Philology'. Indeed, the poem's close hints that Christ's descent to dwell among us – and/or the sentence in the Fourth Gospel which describes that descent – may imitate the process whereby language consents to incorporate itself in and for us. Like the loaded gun of one of Dickinson's most elliptical poems, 'My Life had stood – a Loaded Gun' (754), the living Word 'Has not the power to die'. The incarnate Christ is thus something like a poem; and, if we recall that Emily's 'life' was the loaded gun, it looks as if Christ, the Word incarnate, is also something like Emily.

In this bewildering array of Dickinson's biblical appropriations, we can locate three strategies, exemplary of women's biblical appropriations from the nineteenth century to the present. First, we obviously have a hermeneutics of suspicion, which concentrates on issues of power and powerlessness. Insofar as she identifies herself as powerless, the poet mistrusts, resists, and attacks the embodiment of patriarchal power – both the being and the text. Yet at other moments she lets the text stand for pleasure, eroticizing it by inserting herself into the story, by identifying its spiritualities with her own sensualities, and by feminizings of the divine. In contrast with the hermeneutics of suspicion we might call this the hermeneutics of desire: one finds in the text what one desires to find, one bends it to one's wish.[15] This is, of course, no more than what biblical exegetes have been doing throughout the history of exegesis. But there is something else to Dickinson's method, which I will call a hermeneutics of indeterminacy, and which lends itself prophetically to postmodernist methodologies.[16] What I mean is that we are aware, when reading any of Dickinson's readings of a biblical text, that an act of interpretation is occurring which may be immediately persuasive yet retains an irreducible element of the wilful, the made thing, the playful poetic fiction: interpretation never collapses itself back into text, never makes what the philosophers call 'truth claims'. Further, when we read Dickinson's poetry at large, we see something larger: that she never worries about contradicting herself, that terms such as 'God', 'Jesus', 'heaven', and so forth, have an abundant variety of meanings, some of them highly ambiguous, many of them mutually incompatible, yet all of them convincing within the local perimeters of the poem. To read Dickinson on God (etcetera), then, is to divest oneself of the desire for a fixed and unitary eternal truth and to accept willy-nilly a plurality of contingent truths. Putting this another way: to the powerless Dickinson daughter Scripture is an antagonist, to the passionate woman Emily it is a lover, to the powerful poet Emily Dickinson it is a poem out of which one makes, of course, other poems.

Dickinson is the boldest of nineteenth-century women poets, surely, because she is the shyest. Since she did not write for publication, she wrote only what passion and intellect dictated. Her nineteenth-century sisters on the other hand labored in a vineyard which required (and inspired) heavy doses of piety and right-thinking, especially in women poets. Outside of Dickinson we don't get the hermeneutics of suspicion, and we don't get the dancing indeterminacies – these are *earnest* poets. Still, if we lift a veil or two we find some rather startling erotic revisionism, for example, in Elizabeth Barrett Browning and Christina Rossetti, as well as some of Dickinson's American contemporaries, for whom Victorian ideas about women's superior morality lead to feminized versions of sacred narratives.

Consider the complicated subversiveness of *Aurora Leigh*. Despite the fact that this is a poem in which

high-minded appeals to God seem to lurk beyond every
second caesura, Browning's poet-heroine Aurora begins by
rejecting Eve's role of 'helpmeet' to her suitor Romney,
claiming the higher vocation of poetry. In an interesting
anticipation of H. D.'s palimpsest figure, the autodidac-
tic (and very didactic) Aurora describes the soul as 'A
palimpsest, a prophet's holograph / Defiled, erased and
covered by a monk's', and culture itself as palimpsestic:
an obscene text beneath which we may yet discern the
'Upstroke of an alpha and omega / Expressing the old
scripture'.[17] The implication is that, by searching her
own soul, the woman poet will discover something equivalent to a sacred writing, beneath layers of cultural
accretions.

Successful as a poet, Aurora fails as a woman, for the
usual nineteenth-century reason that she has not found
true love. Reunited, however, with a worshipful and
physically disabled Romney at the narrative's inspira-
tional close, Aurora assumes the stance of a prophet. Or,
rather, a prophet combined with a woman warrior, as
she seems half Isaiah, half Joshua. As she presses the
clarion to her 'woman's lip' now consecrated by connu-
bial love, her vocation is to 'blow all class walls level as
Jericho' (389). At the same time, Aurora's lower-class
alter ego, the 'sweet holy Marion' (262) of the subplot,
is a combination Virgin and Magdalen. Abducted and
raped, mother of a child whose father is unknown,
Marion's 'holiness' is at first doubted by Aurora just as
Mary's purity is doubted by Joseph in Christian legend.
Nor is this second heroine merely a Madonna. Browning
is at pains to repeat the point that Marion has suffered
a symbolic death from which she can never recover. 'I
was . . . murdered', she says; 'I told you that I waked
up in the grave.' She recounts throwing away a medal-
lion of the Virgin: 'How heavy it seemed!. . . A woman
has been strangled with less weight.' Recovering from
madness, she sees a sunset as 'The great red stone upon

my sepulchre / Which angels were too weak to roll away'
(276–7). Marion is here a Christ lacking the consola-
tions of resurrection. Her inconsolability in Browning's
scheme makes her not less Christlike but more. In the
poem's final trinity of Aurora/Romney/Marion, the slip-
pery Marion is something like a holy ghost.

Veiled in a romance-plot as Browning's conception
may be, it represents a radical female usurpation of
scriptural authority. *Aurora Leigh* feminizes and eroticizes Old Testament prophetic tradition, and hints at
the divinization of a woman who suffers for society's
sins, yet refuses to identify female divinity either with
sexual purity or with suffering. Perhaps most interestingly, the poem serves to relocate sacred history in a
'realistic' secular context. One of *Aurora Leigh*'s critics
worries that 'Milton's organ is put by Mrs. Browning
to play polkas in Mayfair drawing rooms'.[18] In the context of nineteenth-century feminism, with its concern for
social reform, that most patriarchal of literary instruments – Milton's organ – could not have been put to
better use.

Christina Rossetti's 'Goblin Market', a poem whose surface is some degrees more pious than Browning's, is also
perhaps some degrees more subversive. Exploiting the
conventions of ballad as *Aurora Leigh* exploits those of
blank verse narrative, 'Goblin Market' bites off the whole
plot of the Bible: it is a feminized version of temptation,
fall, and redemption. Instead of Adam and Eve, the
poem's allegory gives us two sisters in a pastoral. Instead
of a snake, we have a mysterious troop of goblin men
haunting a genitalized glen, who appear and disappear
into the landscape like animalcules or free-floating phalli,
bearing a wicked excess of temptingly exotic fruits.
Their refrain, 'Come buy, come buy', shrewdly brings
the Christian trope of selling one's soul into juxtaposition with the marriage market and the unspeakable

Victorian fact of female sexuality as commodity. When
the adventurous sister Laura gorges herself on fruits paid
for with a lock of golden hair, the goblin men, having
had their way with her, appear no more, and she falls
into a deathly decline for want of another taste. Virtuous
sister Lizzie goes to help and is subjected to a kind of
attempted gang rape by the goblins, who attack her and
smear her with juices while she 'would not open lip from
lip / Lest they should cram a mouthful in'. One does not
at first reading think of this as a crucifixion. But at the
poem's climax Lizzie offers herself to Laura:

> She cried, 'Laura' up the garden,
> 'Did you miss me?
> Come and kiss me.
> Never mind my bruises,
> Hug me, kiss me, suck my juices
> Squeezed from goblin fruits for you,
> Goblin pulp and goblin dew.
> Eat me, drink me, love me,
> Laura, make much of me;
> For your sake I have braved the glen
> And had to do with goblin merchant men'.[19]

Laura obediently 'kissed and kissed her with a hungry
mouth' in a communion feast which gives us a full-scale
female and even quasi-lesbian Christ. In the poem's
moralizing epilogue, wherein Lizzie and Laura years
later instruct 'children of their own' (perhaps produced
parthenogenetically, since there is no sign of any male
in this poem's idyllic female universe save the invasive
goblins), it is Laura who retells the tale, suggesting,
as with the very similar conclusion of 'The Ancient
Mariner', that the poetic voice finds its best habitation
in the throats of fortunately fallen and reformed sinners.
While 'Goblin Market' shows no symptom of being a
protest poem, it appropriates the Christian scheme of
good and evil, sin and salvation, with a theological exact-

ness which far exceeds Browning's relatively loose religiosity. Sandra Gilbert and Susan Gubar have argued that 'Victorian women, identifying at their most rebellious with Satan, at their least with rebellious Eve, and almost all the time with the Romantic poets, were . . . obsessed with the apocalyptic . . . transformations a revision of Milton might bring about.'[20] Still more, one might add, a revision of the Bible itself.

## III

In her autobiographical meditation *The Gift*, H. D. writes: 'There is, beneath the carved superstructure of every temple to God-the-Father, the dark cave or inner hall or cellar to Mary, mère, mut, mutter, pray for us.'[21] Note in this sentence H. D.'s characteristic compression and wit: the image of the fixed, superior, patriarchal structure juxtaposed with an indeterminate inner-or-under feminine space halfway between nature and artifact, the utterance itself gliding seductively from the rationally symbolic to the playfully semiotic. Beneath or within the law of the father, the love of the mother is the spiritual and etymological object of H. D.'s quest in *Trilogy* as well.

The first of her great late poem-cycles, H. D.'s *Trilogy* was written in London during and just after World War II, and takes as its initial condition the bombing of that city. Like T. S. Eliot in *Four Quartets*, H. D. urges a spiritual response to the devastations of personal and political history, though her saving faith is virtually antipodal to Eliot's. For, where he espouses a conservative *via negativa* of self-denial centered on a Christ who is a 'wounded surgeon', she seeks Christ as Lover. And, where Eliot's Christianity is indistinguishable from the church, H. D. combines intense spirituality with an insouciant resistance to religious authority. Buttressed by her Moravian heritage and a lifetime steeped in the study of myth, comparative religion, and the occult, H. D. insists on the continuity of Egyptian, Greek, and Christian divinities. Her Christ will cease to represent 'pain-worship and death-symbol' and be recovered as resurrected avatar of Osiris, her Virgin is one with Aphrodite and Isis, and her Magdalen will be a figure for the poet herself, 'unseemly', 'an unbalanced, neurotic woman' who, in an illustration of the promise that the last shall be first, was 'the first actually to witness His life-after-death'.[22] The three poems of *Trilogy* form an ascendingly feminized and eroticized re-writing of scriptural themes co-ordinated with an increasingly subversive and playful treatment of scriptural texts and traditions. Each poem is an extended meditation interrupted by a dream-vision of which the poet is herself exegete; each dream re-imagines a biblical subject, retrieving it from dogma and cultural fixity, and relocating it within an economy of desire. Their trajectory moves from war and doubt within civilizations and souls, to birth and revelation for both. Dialogic not only with past texts but with a despairing self, with twentieth-century materialism and death-worship, with father-figures who alternately support and condescend, the poem from its outset is dialogic as well with the reader. We are directly addressed, made intimate with the poet's struggles, invited to share her visions, as she reopens the closed Book, reconceives a story we thought was finished.

'The Walls Do Not Fall' (1942–3) begins with an effort to reconstruct the poet's position as sacred scribe, preserver of spiritual truths through aeons of successively destroyed civilizations, despite the murderous and cynical materialism by which she is surrounded:

> Thoth, Hermes, the stylus,
> the palette, the pen, the quill endure,

though our books are a floor
of smouldering ash under our feet.

(9)

Like Dickinson, H. D. seizes on the opening of the
Fourth Gospel, *'In the beginning / was the Word'* (10),
urging the priority of Word over Sword. But, in a radical
swerve from modernism's usual privileging of language
and the consciousness of an intellectual elite, she further
asserts the deeper priority of 'their begetter, / Dream /
Vision . . . open to everyone' (11, 20). Dream needs no
institutional mediator, no authority; it is the Holy Ghost
within the self. Language in the poet's imagery is
feminized, uterized, organicized, as shells and pearls;
what words contain is more important than what they
reveal; they are 'anagrams, cryptograms / little boxes
conditioned / to hatch butterflies' (39). Torn by self-
doubt, she argues that 'my mind (yours), / your way of
thought (mine), // each has its peculiar intricate map'
of 'the eternal realities' (38). Thus H. D.'s redemptive
strategy overtly fuses a hermeneutics of desire with a
hermeneutics of indeterminacy. At the center of 'The
Walls Do Not Fall' the poet's dream of a youthful Osiris-
Christ precipitates a series of puns on 'Osiris/Sirius/O
sire is' which resolve in the *'zrr-hiss'* of the bombs still
falling and the awareness that

> *we know no rule*
> *of procedure,*
>
> *we are voyagers, discoverers*
> *of the not-known,*
>
> *the unrecorded;*
> *we have no map;*
>
> *possibly we will reach haven,*
> *heaven.*

(43)

The play of textual desire accelerates in 'Tribute to the Angels' (1944). At the same time, the poet in this second sequence begins gently to deploy a hermeneutics of suspicion, which until this point she has suppressed. The suspicion addresses itself to the issue of canonization and its capacity to make cruelty and orthodoxy mutually supportive principles. Quoting John of Patmos, the poet juxtaposes his assertion of authority and dogma with the divinely anti-authoritarian utterance of Christ:

> *I John saw. I testify;*
> *if any man shall add*
>
> *God shall add unto him the plagues,*
> *but he that sat upon the throne* said,
>
> *I make all things new.*
> *I John saw. I testify,*
>
> but *I make all things new,*
> said He of the seven stars,
>
> he of the seventy-times-seven
> passionate, bitter wrongs.
>
> (3)

Seizing this textual permission, the poet becomes not merely scribe but alchemist. She transforms language, distilling 'a word most bitter, *marah*, / a word bitterer still, *mar*', in a crucible and flame which represent female and male principles, until the terms for sea-brine and bitterness 'are melted, fuse and join // and change and alter, / mer, mere, mère, mater, Maia, Mary, // Star of the Sea, / Mother' (8). Spliced with this narrative, the poet describes seeing a burnt-out apple tree flowering as by miracle in London 1944. In a gesture which restores the authority of interpretation/revelation from author to reader, she confesses her inability to define the resurrection she has witnessed in conventional terms, but reminds us: 'You have seen for yourself / that burnt-out wood crumbling . . . / you have seen for yourself' (21). In yet another splicing she alters John's apocalyptic plague-dealing angels into a new set of angelic messengers who balance destruction and war with creation and peace, and whom she honors by giving 'thanks that we rise again from death and live'. In each of the poem's strands, H. D. transforms suffering to rebirth.

At the center of 'Tribute', the poet's ritual invocation of an already revisionist set of angels is interrupted by a dream of the white-clad 'Lady' who is and is not a compound of pagan and Christian goddesses, is and is not her iconography. A nameless companion in dialogue with the poet attempts to label the vision, but the poet half-mockingly begs to differ:

> . . . she wasn't hieratic, she wasn't frozen,
> she wasn't very tall;
>
> she is the Vestal
> from the days of Numa,
>
> she carries over the cult
> of the *Bona Dea*,
>
> she carries a book but it is not
> the tome of the ancient wisdom,
>
> the pages, I imagine, are the blank pages
> of the unwritten volume of the new. . . .
>
> but she is not shut up in a cave
> like a Sibyl; she is not
>
> imprisoned in leaden bars
> in a coloured window;

> she is Psyche, the butterfly,
> out of the cocoon.
>
> (38)

The poet pointedly observes that the Lady 'as I saw her' had none of her usual attributes: 'The Lamb was not with her, / either as Bridegroom or Child.' Instead, 'We are her bridegroom and lamb; / her book is our book' (39). Re-empowering the female as psyche, the soul, the poet locates her as well in the world of natural rebirth: for the Lady is also the flowering tree. It is important throughout this sequence to be aware not only of the radically feminist quality of the poet's vision, but of its insistent avoidance of an authoritarian stance. What the poet sees is real, and she refuses to have an interpretation imposed upon her, but by the same token she will not impose upon others. What 'I imagine' is vividly poetic, with a ripple of levity beneath it, but with none of the hieratic and didactic solemnities of Eliot's poem.

In 'The Flowering of the Rod' (December 1944) H. D. writes in a spirit of joy and confidence her own Gnostic Gospel, retelling the story of the woman of Bethany who anoints Christ with precious ointment. Not coincidentally, she has chosen a tale which varies slightly in each Gospel. In H. D.'s version, the woman is the Magdalen; she obtains her ointment from the Magus Kaspar, rigorously trained in a centuries-old hermetic tradition, who surrenders to her both his mystic myrrh and his worldly misogyny. The poet tenderly parodies and reproduces on her own terms the discourses of esoteric learning. 'What she did, everyone knows, / but it is not on record / exactly where and how she found the alabaster jar', she explains (12). 'Some said, this distillation . . . lasted literally forever' (14).

> Some say he was masquerading,
> some say it never happened,

some say it happens over and over . . .
some say he was an old lover
some say he was Abraham,
some say he was God.

(20)

Through the 'unseemly' Magdalen whom he initially
attempts to dismiss, the representative of patriarchal
wisdom experiences a vision of the ancient goddesses
and of the 'scope and plan' of paradise. H. D. mocks as
well the prudery of the conventionally pious, in the figure of the shocked Simon who expresses his irritation at
the erotic scene of the uninvited woman at his party
'actually kissing the feet' of his guest.

Yet more startling is the play of indeterminacy around
the jar of myrrh which the Magdalen both obtains and
is, and which becomes the poem's final focus:

I am Mary, she said, of Magdala,
I am Mary, a great tower;

through my will and my power,
Mary shall be myrrh;

I am Mary – O, there are Marys a-plenty,
(though I am Mara, bitter) I shall be Mary-myrrh.

(16)

Myrrh was for H. D., since her earliest work, a figure for
poetry, and by the time she writes *Trilogy* its significance
is cross-culturally implicate with love, death, resurrection. 'A bundle of myrrh is my well-beloved unto me' in
the Song of Songs; 'he shall lie all night between my
breasts' (1: 13). Myrrh in Egypt was used to embalm the
dead in preparation for the afterlife. The Greek Myrrha
was the mother of Dionysus. According to certain occult
traditions, the Tree of Life was a myrrh tree. Then in
the poem's final words, at the Nativity, when the Virgin

speaks in response to Kaspar's gift, their encounter adds a final meaning:

> she said, Sir, it is a most beautiful fragrance
> as of all flowering things together;
>
> but Kaspar knew the seal of the jar was unbroken,
> he did not know whether she knew
>
> the fragrance came from the bundle of myrrh
> she held in her arms.
>
> (43)

The repetition of the pun Mary-myrrh joins Magdalen, Virgin, the child in the Virgin's arms, and the poem we are completing. Thus H. D. in 'Flowering' implies an ultimate fusion of the virgin-whore with the Christ and with poetry itself. It is an ending curiously similar to the ending of Dickinson's 'A Word made Flesh'. In another sense, however, it is no ending at all but a beginning, a nativity, in which we feel not the satisfactions of achieved closure, but the alternative pleasure of mystery. It is appropriate that *Trilogy* closes with a statement about something that is *not* known. For H. D. wishes to privilege experience above knowledge. At no point does she offer her readings as 'authoritative' or herself as a scriptural 'authority'. Rather, she does what the woman poet must do when confronted with centuries of exegesis: bypassing authority, implying that what 'some say' can never equal sacred truth, she offers the transforming alternative of poetry.

## IV

Among the major Anglo-American women poets of the twentieth century, H. D. is the most profoundly religious, the most seriously engaged in spiritual quest, and the most determined to rescue poetry from secularism.[23] By the same token, she is also the most radically transgressive in her interpretation of the Gospels. For her explicit goal is to recover, in a moment of apocalyptic revelation, as the blasting open of cities in war becomes the blasting open of intellectual and spiritual paradigms, at the heart of the worship of the Father and Son, an older worship of the Mother.

To a woman writing in the last decade of the twentieth century it is an open question whether the work of H. D. will become part of a larger movement to resurrect the goddess whose presence was denied and whose worship was forbidden at the advent of patriarchal monotheism. H. D. has influenced numerous poets concerned with matters intellectual and spiritual, including Robert Duncan, Denise Levertov, Adrienne Rich, and Judy Grahn, and may ultimately be credited with serving as a midwife for the return of the repressed female of whom Freud writes. I would like to conclude this lecture by summarizing what is most characteristic in the revisionist biblical poetry women have been writing in the postwar period, and especially since the sixties. To begin with, it is important to indicate that such work exists in bulk, including not simply countless individual poems, but book-length collections. Second, as one would expect from the synchronicity of second-wave feminism and this period in women's writing, there is an outpouring of explicit anger, indictments of God the Father which go far beyond the subtle critiques of earlier poets. Poems from the point of view of the insulted and injured, the abused and abandoned women in the Bible have multiplied: Eve, Sarah, Lot's wife and daughters, Dinah, Miriam, Zipporah, Jephthah's daughter, the Levite's concubine, Tamar the daughter of David who was raped by Amnon, and so on. There are as well some icy poems from the point of view of Jael and Judith. 'How cruel is the story of Eve', as Stevie Smith says:

What responsibility
It has in history
For cruelty.

Maurya Simon's dialogue between Adam and Eve begins

| EVE | ADAM |
|---|---|
| She said | He said |
|   couldn't we |   why can't you |
| just one more time | for once |
|   dance like the crabs |   be a lady wear |
|     at midnight |     flowers of silk |
|   on the western shores | cover yourself |

and proceeds to delineate a relationship in which female sensuousness triggers male disgust and blame: 'why can't you / remember / remember your crime?' asks Adam. Sylvia Plath overhears the Father and the Son, jealous of nature and women's rotundity, deciding to 'flatten and launder the grossness from these souls'. Her Virgin Mary, recognizing the three wise men as enemies, is terrified by 'the ethereal blankness of their face-ovals'. Her 'Lady Lazarus' sneers at the exploitive savior she calls 'Herr God, Herr Lucifer', who represents the source and rationale for all male condescension, authority, righteousness, and control. Ann Sexton in her mordant retelling of the Gospels, 'The Jesus Papers', depicts the Son as half a performing artist, half an Oedipal cripple obsessed by a loathing for sexuality. She describes the Angel of the Annunciation looking at Mary 'with executioner's eyes', and her God explains how when the Christ is born 'we all must eat beautiful women'. Marge Piercy describes 'the God of the Puritans playing war games on computers'. Celia Gilbert parallels the destruction of Sodom with that of Hiroshima, in a poem which chillingly condemns God the

Father through the mouth of Lot's wife as a 'behemoth in love with death'. Eleanor Wilner's Sarah in the title poem of *Sarah's Choice* instructs Isaac not to go with Abraham; her Miriam – as horrified at the murder of first-born Egyptians as at that of first-born Hebrews – must leave 'one ruler / for another, one Egypt for the next'.[24] Like Dickinson, women writers today commonly recognize the God of patriarchy as an enemy, but the bitterness of their writing belongs specifically to a century which has learned the horror of world war and totalitarianism, and to a feminist analysis which can claim, with Mary Daly, that the religion of patriarchy is a projection of masculine ego, masculine will to power, masculine death-worship.

A second recent development in women's biblical revisionism is a tremendous outpouring of comedy, shameless sexuality, an insistence on sensual immediacy and the details belonging to the flesh as holy, an insistence that the flesh is not incompatible with the intellect. In Diana George's 'The Fall', the poet lets us know that the fruit in question 'was no apple, people', but the banana, 'sidekick and brother / of the snake', and that Adam and Eve 'fell into metaphor'. Linda Pastan's Eve deftly suggests that the story of the rib makes her exemplary of what is 'chosen / To grow into something quite different', thus appropriating the idea of the covenant and of historical process as female. Naming becomes a female act in many women's poems; or, as in Ursula LeGuin's counter-parable 'She Un-Names Them', women reject the categories which obscure animal reality. Exile becomes not a punishment but an escape from a paradise and an Adam whom women poets with startling frequency describe as 'boring'. The embrace of adventure as well as knowledge governs many women's poems. Thus Kathleen Norris invokes Eve as 'Mother of fictions / and of irony. . . . Mother of science / and the critical method . . . Come with us, Muse of exile, /

Mother of the road.' Leda Whitman's Eve 'laughed at his tree, his keep out / sign and electrical fence'. Enid Dame's raunchy and philosophical Lilith, in *Lilith and her Demons*, 'stormed out of Eden / into history', where 'the names they call me / haven't changed / in 4,000 years'. Madeline Tiger's Magdalene, in her *Mary of Migdal* sequence, sexually abused, abused by Donatello's image of her, possessed by demons ('He tells my story, revealing my scars / It is he, in my mouth, calling me whore'), neglected by history, maintains 'the true Eucharist' of her erotic connection with God. Repossessing the maternal language appropriated by the Gospels, a nursing mother in Robin Morgan's 'Network of the Imaginary Mother' says to her infant son, and by implication all infants suffering from hunger and poverty:

> Take. Eat. This is my body,
> this real milk, thin, sweet, bluish,
> which I give for the life of the world.

To insert the female self into Scripture, into history, would mean a transvaluation of values, as Miriam Kessler suggests:

> Where at that Last Supper was a woman?
> Someone to pour the wine,
> a cautionary voice that might have said
> *Take it easy, boys.*
> *This kind of thing could get a fellow killed.*
> A *Seder* without women, kids?
> I'd edit the entire script.[25]

A final development in contemporary women's poetry, perhaps marginal to biblical revisionism, is the 'goddess' poetry connected to the women's spirituality movement.[26] Most of this poetry avoids and evades biblical texts, one might say, like the plague. Its primary sources are pagan, Native American, African, and Hindu. But

its motifs and motivations parallel those of biblical revisionism: the return of immanence and nature, the re-
connection of body to spirit, the rejection of dogma and
the embrace of syncretism, and an insistence on the
unmediated personal experience of the divine. Though
she is not usually listed among the poets of this group,
I would like to conclude by citing Lucille Clifton, whose
lyric confidence enables her to play many sacred parts,
as someone who combines traditions much in the fashion
of H. D. In one of her earliest published poems, Clifton
defines an outrageously female holiness, deploying a
tone that fuses celebration, defiance, and humorous
sympathy for 'the man' whose gods deprive him of grace:

> if i stand in my window
> naked in my own house
> and press my breasts
> against my windowpane
> like black birds pushing against glass
> . . . . . .
> and if the man come to stop me
> in my own house
> naked in my own window
> saying i have offended him
> i have offended his
>
> Gods
>
> let him watch my black body
> push against my own glass
> let him discover self
> let him run naked through the streets
> crying
> praying in tongues[27]

To reveal oneself enables the other to 'discover self',
perhaps to suffer, perhaps to be delivered. If 'All flesh is
kin and kin', as Clifton later writes, her black body might
well serve as Pentecostal miracle to an antagonistic white

man. Clifton has written a sequence of poems to the
black Hindu Goddess Kali in which an assertion of terrifying, dark female power is initially resisted, ultimately
accepted. One may hear Kali behind a sequence of mini-
ature lyrics entitled 'some Jesus', in which Clifton's
voice as a black woman blends with the major figures of
both Testaments, male and female. In 'good friday',

> i rise up above my self
> like a fish flying
>
> men will be gods
> if they want it
>
> (104)

In 'to a dark moses',

> you are the one
> i am lit for.
> come with your rod
> that twists
> and is a serpent.
> i am the bush.
> i am burning.
> i am not consumed.
>
> (127)

In 'the making of poems',

> the reason why i do it
> though i fail and fail
> in the giving of true names
> is i am adam and his mother
> and these failures are my job.
>
> (186)

In another sequence, Clifton tells the story of the
Mother of God as a tale of anticipated suffering: 'at a
certain place when she see something / it will break her

eye' ('the astrologer predicts at mary's birth'; 196). Suffering becomes an almost terrifying bliss in 'holy night',

> joseph, i afraid of stars,
> their brilliant seeing.
> . . . .
> joseph, is wind burning from east
> joseph, i shine, oh joseph,        oh
> illuminated night.
>
> (200)

Ecstasy becomes normalcy, and at last Mary in old age
wonders, 'could i have fought these thing?. . . . could i
have walk away?' (202), and the poet speaks for a chor-
ale of women praying for their sister woman 'split by
sanctified seed' (203). Like the spirituality of H. D., that
of Lucille Clifton is intensified rather than dissipated by
its independence of dogma, its syncretism, and its ability
to represent women as central to sacred drama. In Clifton's most recent book, *Next: New Poems*, 'at creation',

> . . . i and my body rise
> with the dusky beasts
> with eve and her brother
> to gasp in
> the unsubstantial air
> and evenly begin the long
> slide out of paradise.
> all life is life.
> all clay is kin and kin.[28]

Finally, in a poem called 'my dream about God':

> He is wearing my grandfather's hat.
> He is taller than my last uncle
> . . .
> when i whisper He strains to hear me and
> He does whatever i say.

It is a common dream, sprung from an old promise. For the Moses of Exodus exclaims, 'Would God that all the Lord's people were prophets' (Numbers 11: 29). If the Bible is a flaming sword forbidding our entrance to the garden, it is also a burning bush urging us toward freedom. It is what we wrestle with all night and from which we may, if we demand it, wrest a blessing.

## NOTES

1  Wallace Stevens, 'The Noble Rider and the Sound of Words', *The Necessary Angel: Essays on Reality and the Imagination* (London: Faber & Faber, 1951), p. 36.
2  H. D., *Trilogy* (New York: New Directions, 1973), p. 103.
3  Michael Walzer, *Exodus and Revolution* (New York: Basic Books, 1985).
4  Rosemary Ruether, *Sexism and God-Talk: Toward a Feminist Theology* (Boston: Beacon Press, 1983), pp. 117–19. Mary K. Wakeman argues in 'Biblical Prophecy and Modern Feminism' that the Bible in general and the prophets in particular may be read as a paradigm for cultural transformation. Prophecy involves '1) an inner convulsion 2) under pressure of historical circumstances which results in 3) a radical break with prevailing beliefs; that inner convulsion depends on 4) the resurrection of suppressed values (that have in fact underpinned the dominant ethos), and the radical break then results in 5) subversion of the dominating institutional forms 6) including language.' In *Beyond Androcentrism: New Essays on Women and Religion*, ed. Rita Gross (Missoula, Mont.: Scholars Press, 1977), p. 67.
5  See Stevan Davies, *The Revolt of the Widows: The Social World of the Apocryphal Acts* (Carbondale: Southern Illinois Press; London: Feffer & Simons, 1980); *Women of Spirit: Female Leadership in the Jewish and Christian Traditions*, eds Rosemary Ruether and Eleanor McLaughlin (New York: Simon & Schuster, 1979).

6  Elaine Pagels, *The Gnostic Gospels* (New York: Random House, 1979).

7  Joseph L. Blau, 'Tradition and Innovation', in *Essays on Jewish Life and Thought*, eds Joseph L. Blau et al. (New York: Columbia University Press, 1959), pp. 95–104. Katherine Doob Sakenfield, 'Feminist Uses of Biblical Materials', in *Feminist Interpretations of the Bible*, ed. Letty Russell (Philadelphia: Westminster Press, 1985), advocates feminist emulation of the prophets, who revived some forgotten traditions, reinterpreted some others, rejected still others.

8  Edmund Leach and Alan Aycock, *Structuralist Interpretations of the Bible* (Cambridge: Cambridge University Press, 1983).

9  Roland Barthes, 'The Struggle with the Angel', *Image, Music, Text*, essays selected and translated by Stephen Heath (New York: Hill & Wang, 1977), p. 140.

10  Geoffrey Hartman, 'The Struggle for the Text', in *Midrash and Literature*, eds Geoffrey Hartman and Sanford Budick (New Haven: Yale University Press, 1986), pp. 11–13.

11  Robert Alter, 'Introduction' to *The Literary Guide to the Bible*, eds Robert Alter and Frank Kermode (Cambridge, Mass.: Harvard University Press, 1987), pp. 12–13.

12  Gerald L. Bruns, 'Midrash and Allegory: the Beginning of Scriptural Interpretation', in Alter and Kermode, pp. 627, 633 (parentheses mine). Compare Elizabeth Schüssler Fiorenza's politically oriented concept of the 'ecclesia gynaikon' or woman-church as 'the locus or place of divine revelation' which must both 'challenge the scriptural authority of patriarchal texts and explore how the Bible is used as a weapon against women in our struggles . . . it also must explore whether and how the Bible can become a resource in this struggle', and it must claim the authority 'to choose or to reject' biblical texts: 'The Will to Choose or to Reject: Continuing our Critical Work', in Russell, pp. 128–31.

13  Bruns, p. 633.

14  Emily Dickinson, *Complete Poems*, ed. Thomas H. Johnson (Boston: Little, Brown, 1955), no. 1545. Subsequent

Dickinson poems are quoted from this edition and cited by number (given in parentheses).

15   See the careful discussion of this process in Rachel Blau DuPlessis, 'Psyche, or Wholeness', *Massachusetts Review* (Spring 1979), pp. 77–96, a key essay on what women are doing when they interpret a text, especially when they recognize themselves to be at odds with traditional interpretations. Writing on the myth of Eros and Psyche, DuPlessis comes up against Neumann's prior reading which claims that Psyche becomes truly feminine when she prefers beauty to knowledge: 'But this great scholar is wrong. Neumann – wrong. When I say this, I see my father, deep walnut shelves filled with books. . . . I say: I needed this, you needed that. I say: I do not believe your interpretation. But he has studied! and I have not. Yet I know what I want to feel, and I want to make the myth tell me that.' Later, DuPlessis observes, 'By reading I mean an act of reading myself in the text, understanding my hairs, my seeds, my rushing waters, my journey . . . I make my Psyche from my need. And when others need a different Psyche, let them make it.'

16   Contemporary feminist theology, as I read it, makes ample use of the hermeneutics of suspicion and the hermeneutics of desire; that is, feminist theology has occupied itself on the one hand with demonstrating biblical misogyny, on the other with finding in the biblical texts narrative and other material supportive of women and of femaleness. The idea that the scriptural text can (must?) always be plurally interpreted has not yet become popular among feminist scholars, although the principle is well enough understood in modern biblical scholarship. Important exceptions are Mary Callaway, *Sing, O Barren One: A Study in Comparative Midrash* (Atlanta: Scholars Press, 1986); Elaine Pagels, *Adam, Eve and the Serpent* (New York: Random House, 1988); Marina Warner, *Alone of All Her Sex: The Myth and the Cult of the Virgin Mary* (New York: Knopf, 1983); and above all Mieke Bal, in *Lethal Love* (Bloomington: Indiana University Press, 1987), *Murder and Difference: Genre, Gender and Scholarship on Sisera's Death* (Bloomington: Indiana University

Press, 1988), and *Death and Dissymmetry: the Politics of Coherence in the Book of Judges* (Chicago and London: University of Chicago Press, 1988). Bal's recurrent point is that her own readings 'present an alternative to other readings, not a "correct", let alone the "only possible" interpretation of what the texts "really say". Texts trigger readings; that is what they are: the occasion of a reaction. The feeling that there is a text in support of one's view makes texts such efficient ideological weapons', yet 'Every reading is different from, and in contact with, the text': *Lethal Love*, p. 132. My own view strongly concurs. We have all been taught to assume that the Bible is consistent and monolithic. As feminists we should find ourselves urging that the scriptural text is, on the contrary, *not* necessarily monolithic, *not* necessarily coherent, *not* necessarily unified, but riddled with gaps and contradictions and textual ambivalences allowing for plural readings of which *none can ever be definitive*. An insistent heterodoxy is, it seems to me, one of the great strengths of feminist thinking.

17   Elizabeth Barrett Browning, *Aurora Leigh and Other Poems*, introduced by Cora Kaplan (London: The Women's Press, 1978), p. 64. Subsequent passages are quoted from this edition, with page numbers in parentheses.

18   Henry Chorley, *Atheneum*, 22 November 1856, p. 1425. Quoted by Dorothy Mermin, *Elizabeth Barrett Browning: The Origins of a New Poetry* (Chicago: University of Chicago Press, 1989), p. 223.

19   Christina Rossetti, *The Poetical Works of Christina Rossetti*, ed. William Michael Rossetti (London, 1904; rpt London: Macmillan, 1911), vol. I, pp. 3–22.

20   Sandra M. Gilbert and Susan Gubar, *The Madwoman in the Attic: The Woman Writer and the Nineteenth Century Literary Imagination* (New Haven and London: Yale University Press, 1979), p. 205. Two important nineteenth-century pieces of radical biblical revisionism by American poetesses now forgotten are Maria Brooks's *Zophiel, or the Bride of Seven*, a highly eroticized retelling of the Book of Tobit, complete with comparative-religion footnotes which anticipate those of *The Waste Land*, and Elizabeth

Oakes Smith's *The Sinless Child*, whose heroine is both a second Eve and a female Christ figure. See Alicia Ostriker, *Stealing the Language* (Boston: Beacon Press, 1986), p. 214.

21   H. D., 'The Gift' (MS, Beinecke Library), ch. 4, p. 10; quoted in Susan Friedman, *Penelope's Web: Gender, Modernity, H. D.'s Fiction* (Cambridge: Cambridge University Press, 1990), p. 329.

22   H. D., *Trilogy* (New York: New Directions, 1973), section 12. Further quotations are from this edition; numbers in parentheses refer to the numbered sections of the poem. The major work on H. D. as a revisionist poet of the sacred remains Susan Stanford Friedman, *Psyche Reborn: The Emergence of H. D.* (Bloomington: Indiana University Press, 1975).

23   For a discussion of her deliberate undertaking of these projects, as well as her autobiographical account of visionary experiences at Corfu, see H. D., *Tribute to Freud* (New York: New Directions, 1956). H. D. makes clear in this volume her quarrel with secular rationalism. The figure of the Magus Kaspar in 'Flowering' is based on Freud, with whom H. D. undertook analysis in 1933–4.

24   Stevie Smith, *Collected Poems* (New York: Oxford University Press, 1976), p. 481. Maurya Simon, 'Adam Eve', *Grove Magazine* 1, no. 6 (Spring 1982), p. 44. Sylvia Plath, *Collected Poems*, ed. Ted Hughes (New York: Harper & Row, 1981), pp. 129–30, 148, 246. Anne Sexton, *Complete Poems* (Boston: Houghton Mifflin, 1981), pp. 344–5. Marge Piercy, 'The Emperor', *Circles on the Water: Selected Poems* (New York: Knopf, 1982), pp. 99–101. Celia Gilbert, 'Lot's Wife', *Bonfire* (Boston: Alice James Press, 1983), pp. 65–71. Eleanor Wilner, *Sarah's Choice* (Chicago: University of Chicago Press, 1989), pp. 21–4, 8.

25   Diana George, 'The Fall', *The Evolution of Love* (Grenada, Miss.: Salt-Works Press, 1977). Linda Pastan, 'Aspects of Eve', *Aspects of Eve* (New York: Norton, 1975). Ursula LeGuin, 'She Un-names Them', *Buffalo Gals and Other Animal Presences* (Santa Barbara, Calif.: Capra Press, 1987). Kathleen Norris, 'A Prayer to Eve' (unpublished manuscript). Leda Whitman, from 'Overheard in the

Garden and Elsewhere', unpublished manuscript. Enid Dame, 'Lilith', 'Lilith Talks About Men', *Lilith and Her Demons* (Merrick, NY: Cross-Cultural Communications, 1986), pp. 4, 10. Madeline Tiger, *Mary of Migdal* (Galloway, NJ: Still Waters Press, 1991). Robin Morgan, 'Network of the Imaginary Mother', *Lady of the Beasts* (New York: Random House, 1976), pp. 63–88. Miriam Kessler, 'Last Supper', unpublished manuscript.

26  A good anthology is *She Rises Like the Sun*, ed. Janine Canan (Freedom, Calif.: Crossing Press, 1989). See also Judy Grahn, *The Queen of Wands* (Trumansburg, NY: Crossing Press, 1982) and *The Queen of Swords* (Boston: Beacon Press, 1987).

27  Lucille Clifton, *Good Woman: Poems and a Memoir 1969–1980* (Brockport, NY: BOA Editions, 1987), p. 25. Subsequent poems (with page numbers in parentheses) are quoted from this edition except where noted.

28  Lucille Clifton, *Next: New Poems* (Brockport, NY: BOA Editions, 1987), p. 22. The following poem is quoted from this volume as well.

# The Lilith Poems

*for Enid Dame and Grace Paley*

## 1 LILITH TO EVE: HOUSE, GARDEN

I am the woman outside your tidy house
And garden, you see me
From the corner of your eye
In my humble cleaning lady clothes
Passing by your border of geraniums
And you feel satisfied
You feel like a cat on a pillow

I am the woman with hair in a rainbow
Rag, body of iron
I take your laundry in, suckle your young
Scrub your toilets
Cut your sugar cane and
Plant and pick your cotton
In this place you name paradise, while you
Wear amulets and cast spells
Against me in your weakness

I am the one you confess
Sympathy for, you are doing a study
Of crime in my environment, of rats
In my apartment, of my
Sexual victimization, you're raising money

To send my child to summer camp, you'd love
If I were not so sullen
And so mute

Catch me on a Saturday night
In my high heels stepping out and you shiver
I have the keys to your front door
In my pocket

## 2  LILITH JUMPS THE FENCE

Girl, that man of yours
Was one pathetic creature
Puffing his chest, thinking the world of himself,
Standing there saying *Lie down* and *hold still*,
Waving his sceptre at the jacaranda,
The bougainvillea, like the boss of something,
Though wasn't he only taking orders
From a bigger boss,
Or pulling stones from the ground to set on top
  he'd say *We need this wall*,
Of other stones
Paradise constantly in
Motion, and him wanting it to stop –
What kind of husband
Was that, what kind of lover?

Honey, I answered
No hard feelings, but I don't like men
Who try to lay down the law
And I don't like enclosures
Nobody gives me orders
Now or ever

They say he invented names, and it's true
He called me shrew, bitch, witch,
And dumb cunt, he was that scandalized
Spilled a mouthful of curses
When I jumped that fence
Then God put him to sleep and gave him you

## 3  LILITH DECONSTRUCTS SCRIPTURE

And God saw that
You were go/o/d and

Told him your name
Was wom/b/an, a flesh
Section
A man/made
Abject object
Of his affection

Told him your name
Be quiet

*You don't know you have*      *Eve*
This curse, discourse
*You are a mother*
*Tongue*
The cause, the –
Ology the pre –
Text, the testament a
Testicle
To protect it is
Logical                          *you don't know you have*
                                 *you are a mother*
                                 *tongue*

Let us be object/ive:
To hate, to penetrate
To legislate, and to
Enumerate, that is his
Temporary fate:

What's the appeal          *you m/other*
Of the apple:              *of all living*
Take a bite, take a        *might    re/member*
Byte
And find out?

## 4  LILITH UNVEILS HERSELF

He thinks me evil, he be
Afraid of me and always desiring me
Chasing my black behind and my woolly black hair
But it's you I'm after,
Girl,
In the dark when I slip between
The two of you, whispering and touching
Laughing in your ear, I know
The man causes you pain but you stay faithful,
The man is boring but you pay attention,
The man some cardboard heart and you a mother
Watching your children hurt one another

I know
How you feel, I bear a hundred
Babies every day, and they die by nightfall
The man tells you to call them
Demons, to him it is nothing if they die,
But every midnight I kiss
Their dead faces
And then I creep into your house
With my smell of ripeness
With my smell of corpses, with my
Ancient angers
You feel me squeeze between you and the man
I hug your body, girl, I breathe
*Have courage*

# 5  LILITH SAYS WHERE TREES COME FROM

Changing the language is
Not easy you don't
Just disrupt
It you got
To raise it, raise it up but
What with?/ what with the
Weeds pushing
Busting with lust
Up between the cement
Cracks of our dirty sidewalks and what with
Their perfect stems and leaves their
Grace their goings
To seed and the stone
Crumbling up some more then

Pretty soon soil appears on
Some kind of time-scale
Which is not our business
How long it
May happen to take?/ just
We keep pushing
Child, we keep dropping
The seeds

And being part of mystery that is
Bigger than language
And changes the language
And bursts it apart
And grows up and
Wildly away out of it

## 6   LILITH'S NEW SONG

Now clap your hands for this new song
Now sing it –
Here she comes
Yemanja
Here she comes
Seboulisa
Here she comes
Oshun
Here she comes
Innanna
Here she comes
Astarte
Here she comes
Ishtar
Here she comes
Kali
Here she comes
Gaia
Here she comes
Shekhinah
Here she comes
Mary
Here she comes
Spider Lady
Queen of Heaven and Earth
Queen of Ocean and
Big Queen of the Underworld
Now sing it
Now sing it
Ooooweeee
Doowaa
Shoobadoo-oo
Now clap those hands
And stamp those feet
And sing it!

NOTE ON LILITH

According to Jewish legend, the first woman created to
be Adam's wife was Lilith. Adam and Lilith quarreled
immediately because she refused to lie beneath him,
claiming she was his equal because they were both made
of earth. When Adam refused to listen to her, Lilith
pronounced the ineffable name of God and flew out of
Eden. Adam complained of her escape to God, who sent
three angels to fetch her back. The angels found her in
the Red Sea, consorting promiscuously with demons,
and demanded she return. When she would not go with
them she was cursed: she would have to give birth to a
hundred demons every day, and they would die by nightfall. It is said that Lilith attempts to seduce men, and
that she slips between a man and his wife to steal drops
of his semen and make demons from it to plague man-
kind. Traditional households protected themselves from
Lilith with amulets and spells.

# Transactions/Transgressions: An Interview with Alicia Ostriker

*conducted by Catherine Pastore Blair and Harold Schweizer*

**SCHWEIZER** In 'Tradition and the Individual Talent', T. S. Eliot claims that the really new work of art slightly alters tradition. How really new is women's poetry and what are the changes it has brought about?

**OSTRIKER** Ecclesiastes tells us that there is nothing new under the sun. Perhaps we should rest content with that. Yet we know that movements occur in the history of art and literature, even if we can neither date nor define them very precisely. While writing *Stealing the Language* I had Eliot's marvelous essay precisely in mind. I have always pictured Eliot's 'tradition' as an infinitely expandable heavenly dinner party, at which, when the new guest arrives, everyone stirs around the room a bit and the conversation changes slightly. James Merrill evidently imagines something similar in *The Changing Light at Sandover*. The premise of *Stealing the Language* was that what applies to the single new work or single new poet must also apply to collective events, movements in literature. When the 'genuinely new' appears, the old order rearranges itself to accommodate it; the meaning of the past alters at the advent of the new. I was thinking also of Rimbaud's desperate cry for 'quelque chose de nouveau' in a stifling world. The question I addressed was, then, what constitutes the newness of women's poetry in the post-sixties period? What happens here that never happened in literature previously? Can it be defined – that collective voice?

I tried to answer this question on the basis of reading approximately two hundred individual volumes of poetry by women in the post-sixties period, and perhaps a dozen anthologies. My method was radically inductive: I began with some rather sketchy hypotheses, which changed in the course of the reading, as I permitted the poetry to reveal its patterns rather than imposing the grid of prior theory on it. What I concluded can be briefly summarized, although such a summary cannot convey the emotional and intellectual intensity of the poetry itself.

The 'newness' of women's poetry is most clearly and conspicuously thematic. Women strive toward autonomous self-definition as women, which should be no surprise, since they have been defined by patriarchy for four thousand years. They write of the struggle against gendered muteness, gendered invisibility, and their own sense of being divided selves. They write of the body's previously taboo realities including menstruation, sexuality, pregnancy, childbirth, the nursing of children, the horror of incest and rape, the facts of aging and illness, the absurdity of the cult of 'beauty'. They explode with anger at the entrapment of gender roles and at their own helpless complicities. Then they explode with erotic desire that is very different from conventional male desire, as it insists not on conquest but on intimacy, and ripples out to include every relationship, and on into the body politic. Finally, they write revisionist mythology, invading past tradition in order to change it. In order, as Adrienne Rich says, 'to break its hold over us'. I do not of course claim that all women poets do all these things. Rather, here is what women are doing that extends the prior range of poetry.

Another, more shadowy set of questions is formalist. If form is never a fixed quantity but always an 'extension of content', as Robert Creely I think correctly puts it, how can we describe the difference women's poetry makes in formal, stylistic terms? Our critical vocabulary is extremely meager regarding prosody, tone of voice, and structure in poetry, notwithstanding the popularity of the term 'poetics', which tends to mean everything and nothing. We know almost nothing about poetic form, especially in the modern age, and less than that about the interface between form and meaning. The French feminists, for example Cixous, argue that 'defining a feminine practice of writing is impossible', that it can't be theorized, which, as she says, doesn't mean it doesn't exist. For Kristeva, femaleness is itself inexpressible in language, the female writer can only be negative, disruptive, semiotic instead of symbolic, she can never properly enter language. I think this is nonsense. I stand with those who see language as inexhaustibly multiple, full of change and layering and contradiction, rather than with those who see it as monolithic. It may be that most forms of academic discourse are 'phallic', or dominated by masculine authority. But even these dominations are never absolute and complete, and the turbulent vastness of language – written, spoken, whispered, shouted, muttered, sung, in the kitchens and bedrooms, streets and marketplaces of the world – can never be reduced to the laughably tiny rigidities of institutional discourse. Who would dream of such a thing but a professor, trying to reproduce the world in his own image? Kristeva doesn't bother to read women writers, so how would she know whether the female is or is not expressible?

Literary language, at least in our own time in America, is almost infinitely malleable. Theoretically, we should expect to find women's poetry making formal as well as thematic discoveries. Provisionally, I do find certain fascinating stylistic gestures in women's poetry. For instance, there is what I called the exoskeletal style conspicuous in poets like Plath, Atwood, and Wakoski. Something in the tone of such poets is hard, resistant, addresses the reader as a possible antagonist, simultaneously demands and rejects closeness. The exoskeletal style is a contemporary equivalent of the armor images in poets like Marianne Moore; more overt, it signifies a stance of fierce self-protection and aggression, which I don't recall ever hearing before in the English poetic tradition. A related difference is that women's poetry, far more than men's, provocatively manipulates the space between poem and audience, making it elastic rather than fixed. You, you the reader, are constantly being addressed, commanded, seduced, screamed at, and loved. It's as if the intensity of Baudelaire's 'hypocrite lecteur' were sustained not for one line but for whole poems at a time, with that shocking electricity. Of course this disturbs critics when the distance becomes too close, when the hot breath of the poem gets their glasses steamy and makes it impossible for them to retain their so-called objectivity, or when the poem is structured as a transaction and doesn't want to pretend to be an artifact. I also argue that women poets far more often than men operate to violate – or play with, or dissolve – dualistic categories. Distinctions of mind/body, personal/public, sacred/profane, self/other, are not neutral but oppressive to women writers. So they transgress them – in practice, not merely in theory. Philosophically, the implications of women's opposition to dualism are tremendous, incalculable; they would turn our whole conception of reality upside down. Irigaray of course argues this point too. And there is women's laughter, which, again, feels like an uncomfortable novelty even though it has existed at least since Aphra Behn. All these stylistic features may be traced to the woman writer's contradictory status, simultaneously inside/outside dominant culture. Or they may be traced to the possibility that female identity formation produces a fluid or

permeable self–other boundary, as numerous psycho-
logists including Nancy Chodorow and Carol Gilligan
would argue. But these observations are rather sketchy,
not systematic enough. I'd like someday to come back
to issues of form in women's writing – or encourage my
students to do it, which would save me the trouble. I
should say that I do not think experimental or avant-
garde writing *per se* is feminist, necessarily. Formalist
disruption such as James Joyce's can be assimilated with
no trouble by a phallic literary economy.

**BLAIR** I particularly want to concentrate on you as a
feminist – or writing woman – about where you see
yourself fitting into feminism and where you see it going.
I'd like to proceed somewhat chronologically by going
back to your work on Blake and to ask you if you see a
continuity between that and your later, more obviously
feminist work, in either poetry or criticism. To put it
another way – what do you think Blake has to say to
feminists?

**OSTRIKER** Blake's influence on me was crucial. I describe the ups and downs of our relationship – which has
been like a long marriage or love affair – in the essay
'The Road of Excess: My William Blake'. Since Blake
and I had our little quarrel over his misogyny and I
moved out, we've been rather excellent friends. His con-
genital anti-authoritarianism encourages my own. I attempt, like him, to understand where and how the
structures of oppressive authority work within culture,
and to hear the clanking of the mind-forged manacles.
At the same time I attempt to locate in the culture of
the past – that very same culture – its liberating imaginat-
ive vitality, that secret torch that passes from hand to
hand across the centuries. So part of what I take from
Blake is a double stance toward tradition, an awareness
of its duplicitous forces and possibilities. Another part

is his boundless love of energy, the idea that energy is eternal delight, that exuberance is beauty, that the imagination is divine. Then there is Blake's utopianism and insistence on social justice. And his open exploration of sexuality. And the centering of everything in visionary experience. And the way all these qualities in Blake produce writing so terribly experimental that it couldn't be read as poetry in its own time. Blake died in 1837, surrounded by literary incomprehension and condescension; the first critical book that makes any sense of his poetry is Foster Damon's *William Blake, His Philosophy and Symbols* in 1924, almost a hundred years after Blake's death. 'I must create a system or be enslav'd by another man's', Blake proclaimed. Having studied Blake prepares me both to emulate his daring in my own writing, and to perceive the artistry in transgressive writing by others. I can look at women's writing and see how, where it appears most untraditional, it may actually represent the unacknowledged growing tip of tradition.

**BLAIR** I find *Stealing the Language* exhilarating because of the copious quotations from women's poetry, and I know that you meant it to have this effect, that you say in the preface you want readers to experience the shock of pleasure that will draw them into further investigations of women's poetry. And the quotations seem in a way the best argument for the worth of women's poetry.

You do have other arguments for women's poetry in the book that I would like to ask you about. Sometimes you seem to defend it on traditional grounds – for instance, showing that women can write large philosophical poems. And sometimes you point out differences, such as duplicity or anger. And these strategies place you right in the middle of one of the arguments among feminists. Do you think it's important to argue for a new scale of values for women's poetry or to argue for its worth on the old scale? Should we be establishing difference or similarity?

**OSTRIKER** The choice between 'difference' and 'similarity' is one of those false choices proposed by phallogocentric logic which we should reject. Women are both similar to men and different from them. Shouldn't that be obvious to anyone who hasn't been brainwashed? Likewise our writing both resembles and deviates from men's writing. We need to be able to see both likeness and difference, just as the universities need both courses in women's literature which address feminist issues and courses which address 'mainstream' women's writing. We need both/and, not either/or. Otherwise we have continued ghettoization, continued condescension. The same is of course the case with African-American writing, Native American writing, and so on. The reification of female difference which occurs in both French and Anglo-American feminist theory – making difference an absolute rather than a relative term – merely mirrors the ancient male tactic of turning woman into the Other, the Object. I am amazed that women still fall for this tactic. It perpetuates the slave mentality, the status of woman as victim. And the same damage is done by social constructionists as by essentialists. So your question is a tremendously important one, and goes right to the heart of where feminists need to examine their own assumptions.

The literary strategies of anger and duplicity which I discuss in *Stealing the Language* are in fact examples of strategies which are not at all unique to women writers. Woolf claims that anger is a defect in women's writing; the idea is that art and anger are incompatible because art is supposed to transcend mere human emotion. In that case, what about the anger of Pound and Lawrence? What about the anger of Dante and Swift? Again, while trying to understand the strategy of duplicity in Emily

Dickinson, I suddenly realized that the most duplicitous of poets was not a woman but John Milton. Duplicity is by no means confined to females, but occurs whenever a great artist urgently needs to express something forbidden by the internal censor. In Dickinson's case the lust for power and fame were forbidden, because she was a nineteenth-century maiden lady; in Milton's case the joy of rebelling against a tyrannical God was forbidden, because he was a seventeenth-century Puritan. Duplicity is the art of conveying contrary messages within the same poem, of covertly affirming what one overtly denies, so that denial and affirmation carry an equal charge. 'Aye and no too is no good theology', says King Lear. But it can be great art. These are perfect instances of how the new thing in art – *gendered* anger, *gendered* duplicity – enables us to see the anger and duplicity already embedded in tradition. The meaning of tradition thus changes forever, in exactly the sense Eliot intended.

As to the copiousness of the quotations from women's poetry in *Stealing the Language* – yes, I quote extensively, extravagantly, and I feel vindicated in this because I have received extensive thanks from readers. The plan of offering a wide variety of quotes, of poetic personalities, paid off because the intention was for each of those poetic personalities to find its readers, the ones who would like to know this poet exists. 'Thanks to you I read Elizabeth Bishop.' 'Thanks to you I discovered Sharon Olds.' Or Sexton, or Swenson, or Shange, or whoever. That gives me deep gratification, the sense that I have been a successful matchmaker between poets and readers. I am gratified as well when readers thank me for my copious footnotes which they then use to pursue their own critical concerns.

But back to the question of poetic standards, aesthetic standards. I take this matter very seriously. More seriously than some of my attackers do. In fact, I find that most conservative critics, however loftily they speak of aesthetic principles about which 'everyone' agrees, really haven't a clue what those principles are. If you ask them, they merely bluster. It's the radicals, because they advocate what has not yet been accepted, who are obliged to think seriously about principles. How then can we respond to what looks alien when it first appears? Is there any more basic question – in art history or in humanity? It seems to me I judge and would like to judge the new in poetry, whether it's women's poetry, Native American poetry, or Martian poetry, by the same standards as I judge the old. But I add the proviso that my taste is eclectic. I don't like only one kind of poetry; I try my best to like every kind of excellence. 'One law for the lion and the ox is oppression', as Blake says. So I enjoy the excellent wisecrack as well as the excellent sublime. And all points between.

Ideally, the critic should cultivate as broad a taste as the entire past productivity of the art requires. Only through tremendously rich reading do you discover that many different kinds of beauty, in fact, exist. They do not need to cancel each other, or be treated as mutually exclusive alternatives. As Irigaray reminds us in another context, we do not need to accept the tyranny of the One and the Same. I enjoy poetic elegance, but I also enjoy certain kinds of crude power. I'm obviously fond of satire – but many critics are so refined, so devoted to aesthetic purity, you'd think they never heard of brutes like Wycherley or Rochester.

In the last twenty years the one sort of poetry I feel myself inadequate to evaluate is poetry composed for oral performance in a communal setting, rather than for the printed page. I mention this problem in passing, in the essay 'Dancing at the Devil's Party'. I don't have enough personal experience with this tradition, which is of course an ancient one, to be able to make judgements. Doubtless oral poetry has its own rules of excellence, which make one poem permanently valuable and another only temporarily interesting. But I have not a clue what those rules would be. Of course, neither does any academic critic! So a little humility would be in order here – a little awareness that oral poetry, poetry as performance, predates written poetry by several thousand years.

**SCHWEIZER** As far as taste and standards go, however, I feel that there is a certain sense of exclusion in *Stealing the Language*, in the sense that you only speak about those poets who thematically fit into the thesis of the book. In other words, you do not mention poets like Tess Gallagher, for example, who do not overtly address the questions that your feminist thesis raises. How do you explain these exclusions?

**OSTRIKER** Many poets and passages I admire are not quoted in *Stealing the Language*. The book would have tripled in size if I'd included every quote I thought relevant. What I had to exclude was heartbreaking – beautiful, eloquent, brilliant poems for which there was finally no room.

Tess Gallagher, for example, is a lovely instance of what I call the imperative of intimacy in women poets, discussed in chapter 5 of *Stealing*. Think of how tenderly and empathically she describes not only personal relations but family and community, those concentric circles. Think of the power of relationship as a motif throughout her work, how it bonds, bends, how it extends backward in time. Think of the title poem of her first book, *Instructions to the Double*, and how finely that fits my chapter on questions of identity and the double self. Think of how one poem in that first book is called 'Breasts', and how she addresses her breasts intimately as 'swart nubbins', 'little mothers', and 'good clowns', and how she makes the living, fleshly body present throughout her writing. Like many other poets unfortunately not included in my book, Tess fits my 'feminist thesis' beautifully. A problem I was unable to surmount was the need to choose relatively brief quotations to illustrate my points, with the result that the book is biased toward the epigrammatic rather than the expansive. There are poets who create effects in an accretive and gradual way; to illuminate their meaning you must quote two dozen lines at a time. Since I couldn't fill the book with extended quotations, I had to go for the short shots. In my writing on individual poets, in *Writing Like a Woman*, and in my essays on Blake and other male poets, I am of course able to quote at length.

**SCHWEIZER** If we could stay with *Stealing the Language* for just another moment. In the last pages of that book you claim that 'subjectivity may be as severe and demanding a discipline as objectivity'. But the terms of your claim, that a discipline ought to be severe and demanding, still suggests that you would want both subjectivity and the standards of objectivity. So the result is not a radical subjectivity, but rather subjectivity in the guise of objectivity, a subjectivity with all the badges and reputations of a long tradition of self-denial.

**OSTRIKER** In a sense that is right. Yet the subjective and objective differ on the surface. Probably that is why I oscillate between writing criticism and writing poetry. Why choose between subjectivity and objectivity when humanity demands both? Poetry and criticism are both disciplines, but criticism is inflected more toward a surface appearance of objectivity, in which one's subjectivity remains relatively less enunciated, even though it underlies one's entire work. The critic's personal passions and obsessions fuel any critical writing that is worth a damn; but these passions, obsessions, needs, tastes, whatever, must shape themselves as public discourse. In poetry, the obverse is the case. One's overt subjectivity conceals the rigor, the persistent examination – not to mention the craft required to translate emotion into language. To nail it down. All of that must be disguised in work which wants to appear immediate and spontaneous. You know what Yeats says in 'Adam's Curse': 'A line will take us hours maybe, / But if it does not seem a moment's thought, / Our stitching and unstitching has been naught.' Of course Yeats is bragging a bit; he could revise a poem not for hours but for years, as he did with 'Leda and the Swan'. In the same way as we can labor our whole lives at the discipline of producing the momentary – the illusion of the instantaneous, the foam on the wave – so we can work at the discipline of subjectivity.

Beginning poetry students think they're being personal when they are doing nothing but reproducing the banalities of the culture. They do not write, but are written, in just the sense that Derrida and company claim is true for all of us. They mistake themselves for the clichés of their historic moment and social class. They don't yet know what it means to be personal, to have an interior self, or rather selves, they don't know how impersonally and with what energy and cruelty you have to engage in the art of introspection to start arriving at what is authentically deep, which is always a tumult, shifting sands, never simple. They don't know how to push past the censor – the interior censor that stands at the threshold of every important truth about ourselves, forbidding us to enter, like the guard in Kafka's 'Before the Law'. And they are unaware of that self-censorship, they are timid without being conscious of their own timidity. Look around you: people are so incredibly afraid to encounter their actual interior selves. They prefer not to know. We are all taught to be unconscious; therefore becoming conscious is hard labor. That is the premise of psychoanalysis, and the poet is far more bold than the psychoanalyst. 'A book should be an axe for the frozen sea within us', as Kafka also says.

Yet I do not identify the discipline of subjectivity with self-denial. Far from it. Eliot quotes Hulme on Baudelaire: 'Man is essentially bad; he can only accomplish anything of value by discipline.' That is precisely the opposite of what I mean by discipline, which I take in the sense of focus, pursuit, aim, goal, concentration. Not the discipline of the monk who hates the body, but the discipline of the athlete or the dancer who urges it to achieve its potential force.

I should add that, having oscillated all my life between criticism and poetry, I am trying in *The Nakedness of the Fathers*, my work-in-progress, to produce a work in which both these modes go on simultaneously and interact. Layers of biblical textuality come into play with layers of my own identity and family history; I interpret the Bible, while it interprets me. Absolutely no room in this work for a distance between self and text, or the false duality of subject and object. We intermingle and bleed into each other.

**BLAIR** I would like to ask you a little bit about that, about this dramatic introduction of the personal into your criticism. You've said that you're suspicious of theory because it interferes with your personal responses which seem to be the source of your critical responses. I have a quotation from you: 'first I see what I love, then I try to understand it.' And you indicate suspicion of ideological discourse because it isn't real and collapses into 'formulaic wallpaper', which I thought was a wonderful image. And so I wanted to ask you what you think the personal really has to offer criticism.

**OSTRIKER** What the personal has to offer criticism is candor. Why not let the cat out of the bag? Let critics admit what we all ought to know: we are, each of us, driven by what we love and despise, fear and need. We are motivated by what disturbs us, by enigmas we crave to solve. None of us would write a word without personal motivation. I suppose even ambition is a personal motivation; the careerist is personally careerist. And let us not forget envy, pride, wrath, and so on. Where would criticism be without the deadly sins? The great critics of the past – Sir Philip Sidney, Samuel Johnson, Coleridge, Shelley, Arnold – were unafraid of personality. It seems to me that I like reading criticism in which the personality of the critic is present on the page, bringing to bear the urgency, the slant, the inflexion of a whole human being. I like that and learn from it. Harold Bloom is an exciting critic for me precisely because of his candor: his personality is contiguous with his theories, both are impassioned and aggressive. Criticism which pretends to be dispassionate I simply mistrust; behind the argument for aesthetics there always lurks a (usually reactionary) politics. Increasing numbers of feminist critics presently find themselves uncomfortable with the disguises of critical objectivity; a recent issue of *lingua franca* (February 1991) has an article on that very subject, the reclamation of the first-person singular by feminists. Barbara Smith did breakthrough work as a black feminist saying 'I' in the late seventies. Cixous in 'Sorties' makes very clear how her childhood as an Algerian Jew shapes her needs and passions as a reader. Recently, you could look at Jane Tompkins's essay 'Me and My Shadow', Rachel Blau DuPlessis's *The Pink Guitar*, Nancy Miller, and Jane Gallop. The point everyone is making is that the public/private dichotomy is a lie, that it doesn't fit what we want to say, that it's a form of blindness.

**SCHWEIZER** How do you teach your students to avoid such forms of blindness?

**OSTRIKER** Let me give an example. I recently used Bakhtin in a graduate course called 'Theories of Female

Creativity', which alternates between theoretical works and works of fiction and poetry. The question asked is always how the theoretical text applies or fails to apply to the artistic text. We began with *A Room of One's Own*, which I love because it covers so much ground so swiftly and eloquently, along with *To the Lighthouse*. Then we read *Madwoman in the Attic* with *The Yellow Wallpaper*, concentrating on ideas of oppression and pathology. After that, it was very entertaining to read Bakhtin's 'Discourse in the Novel' with Maxine Hong Kingston's *The Woman Warrior*. The point was to demonstrate how a brilliant theoretical text by a dead white European male, all of whose literary citations are to other dead white European males, nonetheless marvelously illuminates a novel it was never intended to illuminate – this brilliant piece of heteroglossia by a Chinese-American woman. Look here, I could say, *The Woman Warrior* affirms, confirms the details of Bakhtin's theory even better than Dickens and Dostoevsky do. From there I could go to H. D.'s long wartime poem *Trilogy* and show how, though Bakhtin claims that heteroglossia occurs only in fiction and that poetry is univocal, H. D.'s poetry is thoroughly dialogic and intertextual. I love Bakhtin because his ideas ripple out even more widely than he intended.

I am as eclectic with theory as with aesthetics. I would like my critical taste to be broad, so that I could say nothing critically human is alien to me. But I do exercise, as Emily Dickinson says, 'the right to choose or to reject'. What I tend to reject is methodology, which I take, in criticism, to be a substitute for genuine attentiveness. Methodology does your thinking for you so that you needn't bother doing it yourself, you just apply the formula. Mary Daly's coinage about Christian theology, which she calls 'methodolatry', applies to literary studies as well. Methodology is a form of idolatry, taking the wooden stick for the living god.

**BLAIR** This may be a methodology question then: Gilbert and Gubar seem to identify some of the same things in women's writing that you do. I was thinking specifically about anger. They identify this eruption of anger as one of the marks of women's literature. Toril Moi attacked them for insisting on the female author's anger as the true meaning of the text; she feels that thereby they undermine an anti-patriarchal stance by relying on the author as the so-called transcendental signifier of her text. I was wondering if you thought that's what we are doing when we identify anti-patriarchal anger in women's work. Maybe that's a methodolatry question.

**OSTRIKER** Toril Moi attacks Gilbert and Gubar because they don't 'proclaim the death of the author'. This is ridiculous. The death of the author is a critical fiction which not coincidentally came into fashion just at the moment when women started claiming authorship, as numerous feminist critics have noticed. 'Sorry!' cry the high priests disappearing into their sanctuary as the women approach the portal. 'You can't be an author! Don't you know there aren't any authors any more? You're too late! What a pity!' Similarly, just as women authors start defining themselves without genuflecting to the great Fathers, we are told that 'woman' is that which cannot be expressed in language, thanks to some Lacanian mystification which would be laughable if it weren't taken so solemnly by the acolytes of high theory.

Gilbert and Gubar identify anger as one of the marks of nineteenth-century women's literature. They see this anger as sometimes overt, sometimes covert or 'slant', sometimes unconscious. And this perception, among others, helps generate an astonishing wealth of complex, subtle, brilliant, witty analyses. Then along comes Toril Moi in her theoretical jackboots, claiming that they aren't sufficiently anti-patriarchal. Of course it's she who is reductive and oversimplified, not they. And it is just the same with all the other feminist critics she dismisses for their theoretical lapses. It's she who is behaving like the quintessential old-style patriarchal academic in her insistence on a single correct way to go about things. Feminism isn't single. It's multiple. That is its strength.

On the other hand, I agree with Toril Moi in her call for a less monolithic view of the dominant culture, one which would take into account its own fragmentary and contradictory nature. And I do depart from Gilbert and Gubar in the last two chapters of *Stealing the Language*. Up until that point, I cover ground similar to theirs, examining the consequences of women's oppression and women's silencing, looking at how these matters are encoded in poetry which registers the pain of marginality. But then I shift to thinking about female eros and revisionism. Here I can no longer assume that women are entrapped in an oppressor's language without loopholes. I argue that the woman writer can write from a stance of pleasure, and can intervene in the creation of culture. But I'm writing about the twentieth century, where all of this is much clearer. Other feminist critics I admire who look at women writers as not simply victims are Rachel Blau DuPlessis in *Writing Beyond the Ending* and Patricia Yaeger in *Honey-Mad Women*. And a tremendous influence on my own thinking was Susan Friedman's *Psyche Reborn: The Emergence of H. D.*, which showed in massive detail how H. D. was able to wrestle with Sigmund Freud, and use him in her writing as both an antagonist and an ally. All these writers assume, as I do, a double stance toward the dominant culture. We assume that the language, the culture, one's own experience, are always already so capacious as to make room for female pleasure and female reality. 'Act so that there is no use in a centre', says Gertrude Stein in *Tender Buttons*. We need to recognize women's insouciance as well as women's anger.

**SCHWEIZER** A moment ago you mentioned the term 'the oppressor's language'. It seems to me inevitable to speak a language which is gendered, or which reflects the traditions that have shaped it. I find such a predicament in one of your articles, in which you comment on a poem by June Jordan and where your analysis proceeds from 'an obvious moral' to 'a deeper point' and from there on to 'a real secret'. Is that not the language of sexual penetration? Or of the masculine quest? Is this a Freudian slip, or does this progression of thought from 'obvious moral' to 'deeper point' to 'a real secret' adhere to a perhaps universal pattern? Or, to ask the question differently, how is it possible to escape the oppressor's language?

**OSTRIKER** Ah! I didn't realize I had done this here, used the language of penetration as a metaphor for perception. In 'Entering the Tents' I use an erotic metaphor deliberately, provocatively. Speaking of biblical narrative, I ask: 'What do the stories mean to me and what do I mean to them? I cannot tell until I write. And then each story opens to me, as I climb into and into it. And then each story opens like a flower, and I climb down into its throat.' Well, it's fun to play with the idea of biblical narrative as the flower I'm entering. Emily Dickinson takes the position of the bee raiding the flower now and then. Why not? But in the commentary on the June Jordan poem I wasn't being intentionally sexual. So your question raises my consciousness. But in fact the language of penetration, the idea of a movement from surface to interior, is quite comfortable for me, and not necessarily gendered. Perception, understanding, the quest for meaning – these activities for me announce themselves most commonly through metaphors of *depth* or through metaphors of *penetration*. Never transcendence. The truth is never up above. It is always deep, or within.

By the way, this is another set of metaphorical constructs I inherit from Blake, because it governs so much of his thinking. Blake has a strange geometry, according to which the inside of an object is always more spacious than its surface. 'To see the world in a grain of sand, / And heaven in a wild flower, / Hold infinity in the palm of your hand, / And eternity in an hour' is the most familiar expression of his view of reality. The quatrain sounds simple enough, rather charming. But Blake means it literally. His prophetic poems, especially *Milton*, unpack that seemingly light-hearted trivial figure into a vast panorama full of enclosures which contain spaces vaster than themselves, to explain which you have to fancy a geometry of more than three dimensions – which is what he does. H.D. suggests something similar in her treatment of time and eternity in *Tribute to Freud* and in her theory of palimpsests. Dickinson seems to propose the same idea in the little poem which begins by saying that the brain is deeper than the sea, wider than the sky, and ends by saying the brain is just the weight of God. Most particularly, of course, it is the human mind which for Blake is infinitely spacious. When I use the language of penetration myself, it's because I've experienced, though nowhere to the degree or with the clarity Blake has, this sense of the inside being vaster than the outside. That's why I want to move from what I experience as the surface of a text to the inside of it. Whatever that means!

I really edge on mysticism here. I can't help it. Of course I want to perform the same operation on a poem as on a person. It comes back to the idea of intimacy. But women's erotic poems say the same thing over and over. To love is to enter and be entered, both at once. There is this tremendous thirst for interpenetration between self and other in women's writing, most conspicuous in evocations of sexuality, but also visible in other kinds of writing about relationships. The thirst to penetrate the other and be penetrated by the other – this is women's definition of joy.

And what I thought most interesting and charming, most delightful, was that many women's poems describing the sexual act describe it as that experience in which gender *ceases*. The experience of the self/other boundary becoming porous is also the experience in which my gender, your gender, stops being relevant. Gender is then a sort of husk which the interior temporarily casts off before it has to go back and inhabit that separate and gendered body again. I'm describing this crudely, of course; the poems do it better.

So both here, not quite consciously, and in *The Nakedness of the Fathers* very consciously, I use the figure of penetrating the text as an erotic activity. The further I penetrate, the more I find delight. The figure appears first in 'Entering the Tents', later in 'The Wisdom of Solomon', where it is one of Sheba's sequence of erotic jokes and riddles. I should close by saying that my sense of the pleasure of the text is unlike Barthes's. It is less like conquest, more like mutual discovery.

**BLAIR** Do you see yourself as you have described other women poets as 'engaged in a radical transformation of self and society'?

**OSTRIKER** I see myself as engaged in a radical transformation of self. Absolutely. It is ongoing, and I hope it to continue all my life. I wish I could be more confident that I influence social transformation. What I do with my professional life is write and teach. I'm not an organization person, I don't go to meetings and demonstrations very much. Thus I can merely hope that my work makes a difference in the larger world. It is not something one can calibrate. Many of my students are activists, of course, and I encourage that. I've also had people, strangers, coming up to me at conferences to tell me that my writing changed their lives – one life at a time also matters. But most of all it matters that women bring what is supposed to belong to 'private' life into the public world, in writing, because poverty, violence, sexual abuse are part of women's private lives. War is a woman's issue, a feminist issue, as H. D. makes clear in all her late writing. Our attitude toward nature is a woman's issue, as Susan Griffin makes clear in *Women and Nature*. The fact that we think of God as a man, and of authority and power as naturally male, is a woman's issue. You have no idea how powerful the prejudice still is against awareness of certain distressing realities. A woman recently told me that I was the only critic writing on Anne Sexton's poetry who actually used the word 'incest' to describe the situation of the poem 'Briar Rose'. Everyone else used circumlocutions. Now, that astonished me, and yet it didn't. According to some estimates, perhaps a quarter of the children in this country are victims of sexual abuse, and in some ways the worst part of that abuse is the condemnation to silence. To shame and silence. I try in my writing and teaching to help people kill the censor, to bring into language what has been shut in silence, not to be afraid. Let people be conscious instead of unconscious. I try to write and teach in such a way as to give my readers and students courage to do what they fear to do, say what they fear to say. If I help with that task, if I help make my readers and students more courageous, my work makes some little difference. I'd rather stand with Shelley in the wild belief that poets are the unacknowledged legislators of the world – by which I think he means simply that the ideals of poets ultimately filter into what we call 'progress' – than agree with Auden's sensible opinion that 'poetry makes nothing happen'.

**BLAIR**  I wonder if you would comment on your re-imagining of the Bible, just a little bit. Does it seem to you to be a new direction in feminist reading? It seems such a different enterprise from a book like *Stealing the Language*.

**OSTRIKER**   For me, my biblical work is the natural continuation of the chapter on revisionist mythology in *Stealing*. Obviously it is easier and less risky to re-write pagan myths than to rewrite our own, the Judeo-Christian myths which so much more intimately govern our society and our behavior. If a woman does a revisionist feminist version of Orpheus and Euridice, or of Oedipus and the Sphinx, nobody but a few professors will be offended. But if she says God the Father swallowed God the Mother, back in prehistory? That's quite another story. The feminist who tinkers with biblical narrative puts herself in a position like Salman Rushdie's. She is pitting her own imagination against orthodoxy. I feel this work to be frightening. But it is a continuation. It is the next thing one must do.

Suppose we look at the question purely academically. If we want to know how woman relates to patriarchal tradition, it makes logical sense to go to the Bible, which is the founding text of patriarchy. The Bible is the ulti-mate authority for so many other texts, it has generated so many other texts; and, what is more, we can observe within biblical narrative the actual process of patriarchy constructing itself. We watch the Law of the Father gathering its material and building itself up, bit by bit, layer upon layer. The process is fascinating. If then we can demonstrate that women writers respond not simply and singly but multiply and plurally to the ur-text of patriarchy, then we can also perhaps begin to examine the relation of women to the canon at large, in ways that move beyond the simple assumption that a male text is a woman's enemy.

The idea of a hermeneutics of suspicion comes from feminist theology – Rosemary Ruether, Elizabeth Schüssler

Fiorenza, Judith Plaskow are major figures. And Mary Daly, of course, the mother of us all. In my version of it, the reader reads a text of power through the eyes of the powerless, and responds in a variety of ways which register anger and resentment, the adversarial position. In the hermeneutics of desire the reader finds in the text what she wants it to say. Remember, though, that traditional biblical exegesis is simply an unconscious version of what the feminist does consciously and deliberately. 'Mainstream' interpretation has always embodied the hermeneutics of desire. You see what you need to see. Elaine Pagels examines this process for the early Christian church from the Pauline epistles through Augustine, showing how the relation between church and state does a most marvelous flipflop when Christianity becomes the official religion of Empire.

The hermeneutics of indeterminacy is what seems to me potentially most significant for the future. Suppose we take seriously the rabbinic saying that 'There is always another interpretation'. If this is the case, then my interpretation, yours, his, hers, must always be contingent, never final. There is not and cannot ever be a 'correct' interpretation, there can only be another, and another, and another. Mieke Bal says this in *Lethal Love*: 'Texts trigger readings; that is what they are; the occasion of a reaction.' She adds that 'Every reading is different from, and in contact with, the text.' H. D. in *Trilogy* very clearly lines out what I'm describing, the necessity for plural readings which won't cancel each other.

Human civilization has a stake in plural readings. We've seen this at least since the eighteenth century when the notion of religious tolerance was invented to keep the Christian sects from killing each other. The notion of racial tolerance came later. Most people haven't caught on, though. Most people need 'right' answers just as they need 'superior' races. And groups tend to lose their enthusiasm for pluralism when they are no longer persecuted minorities but become dominant majorities. At this particular moment it happens to be feminists and other socially marginal types who are battling for cultural pluralism. Still, this is an activity we're undertaking on behalf of humanity, all of whom would be the happier, I believe, were they to throw away their addiction to final solutions.

**SCHWEIZER** Is there such a thing as an hermeneutics of laughter? In Eco's *The Name of the Rose*, the quest for such an hermeneutics goes up in flames at the end.

**OSTRIKER** A hermeneutics of laughter. Wouldn't it be pretty to think so? You remember the line at the end of *The Sun Also Rises*, when Brett says to Jake that they could have been so happy. They're in a taxi going down some boulevard somewhere together and Jake says, 'Wouldn't it be pretty to think so?'

**SCHWEIZER** Let me be a little more specific then. In the seventeenth chapter of Genesis, Abraham is said to have fallen on his face with laughter after God tells him that Sarah should bear a son. In the eighteenth chapter Sarah herself laughs, but denies it. Do you see in that account some sense of a judgement on laughter— Sarah's laughter, since she was the one to be rebuked?

**OSTRIKER** I laugh when I read the passage. I always do. I giggle. Because there's such an intimate charm to it. It's like an elbow poking, a little wink, when God knows Sarah's got her ear to the flap of the tent. She's eavesdropping. She's laughing silently, of course. But God, being God, knows she's laughing. Sticks his nose in the tent. 'You were laughing.' 'No I wasn't.' 'But you were.' Cut. And then we go on to the next thing. And that to me is such a comic little vignette, that exchange, that kind of 'Gotcha!' And Sarah denies eavesdropping and he says, 'Don't kid around with me.' It takes the form of a rebuke. But it's a playful rebuke. No harm comes of it. It's divine dialogue as entertainment.

**SCHWEIZER**   In the New Testament, when Mary hears the annunciation of the angel that she should give birth to Christ, there is no laughter. But there is a little bit of a hint that such a conversation as you mentioned between God and Sarah might occur again. Mary asks, 'How is this going to be possible?'

**OSTRIKER**   But then we get the Magnificat, don't we? Scholars would say that the Annunciation to Mary is modeled on the structure of the barren woman narratives in the Old Testament, but with that startling and wonderful variation, of the Annunciation being followed by expansive song.

**SCHWEIZER**   In other words, Mary has the chance to improve on Sarah?

**OSTRIKER**   I'm not sure I can answer this question properly, because I don't read the New Testament the way a Christian does. For a Christian, 'New Testament' follows 'Old Testament' and improves on it. For a Jew, these are simply two different books. We don't call the Hebrew Bible 'The Old Testament', in the first place. It is not old for us, it is contemporary. Reading New Testament as a Jew, I read it as a book which derives and deviates from the Hebrew Bible, not as its sequel. Ultimately, the New Testament settles on its own foundations and offers gender problems all its own, along with its new mythos. The women in the Gospels have very different roles from those in the Hebrew Bible, with less concentration on maternity, on biology altogether, and more on questions of faith and discipleship.

**SCHWEIZER**   Purity?

**OSTRIKER**   Yes, that too. The Hebrew Bible usually locates a female's value in her sexuality and procreativity, with a few exceptions such as Deborah in the Book of Judges. Female value in the New Testament, on the contrary, resides in a woman's asexuality. In her capacity to be non-sexual, hence spiritual. Either of these values might be considered important and either might be considered oppressive. A value becomes oppressive when it is reified into the only possible one by which the person must be defined. Do you see what I mean?

**BLAIR**   Sarah's laughter, as you point out, turns into her son Isaac, who gets named 'laughter'. And in *The Nakedness of the Fathers* you have Isaac working very hard to continue to treat the entire universe as a joke.

**OSTRIKER**   Yes, he is the founding father of Jewish humor. Lenny Bruce and Woody Allen must come from somewhere, and, if you ask yourself who's the best biblical candidate for the ancestor of Jewish humor, it's got to be Isaac. Poor fellow. My essay on Irving Feldman's poetry, by the way, pursues this idea in detail.

But let's go back to the question of women's laughter and transformation. I should retract some of my skepticism. Though I'm not in a position to theorize very subtly here, I think everyone agrees that laughter is always transgressive. The moment of laughter ruptures the principles of authority, whatever they may be. Probably that's why, in the hierarchy of genres, comedy ranks low and epic and tragedy rank high. Epic and tragedy reaffirm the social and political order. Tragedy is always the gesture whereby the protagonist enacts a transgressive impulse and we discover that it fails. Must fail. The hero is destroyed by the will to transgress, whether it is his own personal will or that of the gods or fates. Tragedy is the form which persuades us that rulebreaking cannot succeed; order recrystallizes itself around the corpse of the transgressor. Comedy teaches an equal but opposite lesson. Both of course are true from time to time. Comedy teaches that you can transgress and get away with it. It's the point Northrop Frye made so long ago in *Anatomy of Criticism*. The lightest pun, the merest small-scale joke, implicitly teaches the same lesson that high comedy teaches: that there are ways to break or evade the rules and survive. All societies must have comedy as an outlet at least, just as we all have some version of carnival. But it would be normal for 'high' culture to place comedy 'low' in its scale of values, precisely because hilarity mocks and threatens the existing powers.

Someone with an anthropologist's sensibility might try to correlate the relative rigidity or flexibility of societies with the degree to which they were ready to validate comedy. Americans are rather good at comedy, and no good at all at tragedy. Writers in police states can get very good at irony, as we see by the literature that has come out of eastern Europe.

**SCHWEIZER**   If I may proceed from comedy to tragedy, and from laughter to silence, there is that curious silence of Job's wife in the Book of Job. But then again those who speak in the Book of Job necessarily fail to speak the truth. For all their unbridled speeches, Job's counsellors appear to us as more sympathetic when they fall silent for seven days and nights before they cannot hold their tongues at the sight of Job's suffering. Could one not say then that Job's wife's silence is perhaps a more spiritual, a more authentic response to suffering than either Job's quest for justice or his friends' passion for religion?

**OSTRIKER**   Questions about silence are interesting because silence can be a sign for so many things. I haven't thought about the silence of Job's friends, their long silence before they speak, and what that might signify within the Book of Job. Perhaps it signifies their respect for Job as an alpha male. He is a public figure in their community. He's a rich man. He's a great man. He's a leader. So their silence might be the silence of courtiers around a king or nobleman, or a board of directors around the chief executive officer, or the cabinet around the president. They scarcely know how to cope with his abrupt change of state. But your reading is valid also: Job's suffering is so awesome and shocking that the only adequate response seems to be silence. Then there is another kind of silence, which we find often in women's writing and in texts about women: silence as resistance. Silence as refusal to cooperate or comply.

**SCHWEIZER**   Is that Job's wife's silence?

**OSTRIKER**   I think that's Job's wife's silence. And her minimal speech, 'curse God and die', stresses the silence it punctuates, as a silence of muted anger. Then Job's response to her single sentence tells us that we may indeed read her silence as resistance. For the response is, 'You speak as one of the foolish women speak.' 'You'd better shut up' is how we are to translate that. 'Women should hold their tongues', and so forth and so on. So Job's rebuke of his wife, when she has uttered her one pithy saying, relegates her back to the silence which she then maintains for the rest of the Book and which is her place.

Let us say that the various reactions to Job's affliction map out the possibilities of responses in our world to the actuality of arbitrary human suffering. What are the possibilities? The silence of Job's original 'patient' acceptance; the silence of shock; the silence (perhaps) of satisfaction, for we should admit that we are capable of feeling pleasure at another's pain; the silence of resistance. And then the utterances: the 'curse God and die' of embittered submission; the insistence of Job's friends that he must deserve his suffering, which blames the victim – we're all familiar with that. And finally Job's astonishing protest, his challenge to God, unimaginable in the world until he makes it. This is the creation that the Book of Job is all about. What an invention! Here is the human advance, the moral advance. To protest. To say that divine injustice is intolerable. I don't stand for it. I won't stand for it. I demand to have it explained.

**BLAIR** A final question. I know that you overtly derive your work on the Bible in part from the women's spirituality movement. What do you think that movement has to offer?

**OSTRIKER** Like feminism, the women's spirituality movement isn't one thing. It's many things and includes women both inside and outside the established religions. Within the denominations, one front-line struggle has been for women's ordination. Women need to be admitted to the ministry, the priesthood, the rabbinate. Another involves changing the liturgy. Changing God-language. Women want to worship God the Mother, to be able to say God/She as well as God/He. I think all the feminist theologians agree that a God imagined as purely masculine is nothing but idolatry. Women are inventing new rituals, new ceremonies – for example the Rosh Hodesh ceremonies of many Jewish women's spirituality groups, which are actually a revival of an ancient women's holiday for the New Moon. Liberation theology and feminist theology come together at many points. So do women's spirituality and ecofeminism. Women's spirituality is starting to move into the field of therapy, too – it is being used to help heal and strengthen battered women, for example, and there are starting to be feminist revisions of the spiritual language of the twelve-step programs. A tremendous literature already exists on all of this, and it's expanding exponentially. Further out, there are neo-pagans, witches' covens, Goddess worship in many forms, charismatic leaders like Starhawk and Z. Budapest who are also prolific writers. There's a great deal of attention to African and Native American sources. There's the beginning of new holy texts, like the dialogue between Celie and Shug on the nature of God in *The Color Purple*, which I've already heard quoted in several sermons. For anyone to whom women's spirituality is *terra incognita*, a good place to start reading is the anthology *Womanspirit Rising*, edited by Carol Christ and Judith Plaskow, and its sequel, *Weaving the Visions*. Is there any common denominator in all this ferment? Yes, the sacredness of the body. The need to accept, to experience, the body as holy. We all agree on that.

# Alicia Suskin Ostriker: *A Bibliography, 1964–1992*

*compiled by J. C. Bittenbender and C. H. Cronrath*

## 1964

1   'William Blake: A Study in Poetic Technique', *Dissertation Abstracts* 24 (January–March), pp. 3754–5.

## 1965

2   *Vision and Verse in William Blake* (Madison: University of Wisconsin Press), x, 224 pp.
3   'Song and Speech in the Metrics of George Herbert', *PMLA* 80, no. 1 (March), pp. 62–8.

## 1966

4   'Anti-Critic', *Commentary* 41, no. 5 (June), pp. 83–4 (Review of *Against Interpretation* by Susan Sontag.) Reprinted in *Contemporary Literary Criticism* 31 (1985), pp. 405–6.

## 1967

5   'The Three Modes in Tennyson's Prosody', *PMLA* 82, no. 2 (May), pp. 273–84.

## 1968

6   'Fact as Style: the Americanization of Sylvia', *Language and Style* 1, no. 3 (Summer), pp. 201–12. Reprinted in *Contemporary Literary Criticism* 17 (1981), pp. 348–9. Also reprinted as 'The Americanization of Sylvia', in *Writing Like a Woman* (1983), pp. 42–58. Reprinted in *Critical Essays on Sylvia Plath* (1984), pp. 97–109.

## 1969

7   *Songs* (Poetry) (New York: Holt Rinehart and Winston), 49 pp.

## 1970

8   'The Lyric', in *English Poetry and Prose 1540–1674*, volume 2 in the *History of Literature in the English Language*, ed. Christopher Ricks (London: Sphere Books), pp. 119–36. Reprinted as 'The Lyric: The Poetry', in *The New History of Literature: English Poetry and Prose 1540–1674* (1987), pp. 91–106.

9   'Thomas Wyatt and Henry Surrey: Dissonance and Harmony in Lyric Form', *New Literary History* 1, no. 3 (Spring), pp. 387–405.

10  Review of *Blake in the Nineteenth Century: His Reputation as a Poet from Gilchrist to Yeats* by Deborah Dorfman, *Victorian Studies* 14, no. 1 (September), pp. 113–14 (special issue on 'The Victorian Woman').

## 1971

11  'Cry Wolf', *Partisan Review* 38, no. 3 (Summer), pp. 355–8 (Review of *Radical Chic & Mau-Mauing the Flak Catchers* by Tom Wolfe). Reprinted in *The Critical Response to Tom Wolfe* (1992), pp. 51–3.

12   'Other Times, Other Voices', *Partisan Review* 38, no. 2
     (Spring), pp. 218–26 (Review of *Baby Breakdown* by
     Anne Waldman, *At Terror Street and Agony Way* by Char-
     les Bukowski, *The Naomi Poems: Corpse and Beans* by
     Saint Geraud, *A Probable Volume of Dreams* by Marvin
     Bell, and *The Dancers Inherit the Party* by Ian Hamilton
     Finlay).

## 1972

13   'Dinner at Elaine's', *Esquire* 76, no. 4 (April), pp. 93,
     202, 204.
14   'Of Being Numerous', *Partisan Review* 39, no. 2 (Sum-
     mer), pp. 270–5 (Review of *Black Feeling, Black
     Talk, Black Judgment* by Nikki Giovanni, *Livingdying*
     by Cid Corman, *Earthworks* by Sandra Hochman, *Col-
     lected Poems* by Alan Dugan, and *Places to Go* by Joanna
     Kyger).
15   'Weapons and Words', *Partisan Review* 39, no. 3 (Sum-
     mer), pp. 464–8 (Review of *Obscenities* by Michael Casey,
     *Saigon Cemetery* by D. C. Berry, *Treasury Holiday* by
     William Harmon, and *Nuclear Love* by Eugene Wild-
     man).
16   'Norman Mailer and the Mystery Woman', *Esquire* 78,
     no. 5 (November), pp. 122–5.

## 1973

17   'What if We're *Still* Scared, Bored, and Broke?' (on Erich
     von Däniken), *Esquire* 80, no. 6 (December), pp. 238–40,
     328–30.
18   'Poem Objects', *Partisan Review* 40, no. 1 (Winter), pp.
     95–107 (Review of *Concrete Poetry*, ed. Mary Ellen Solt,
     *Anthology of Concrete Poetry*, ed. Emmett Williams, and
     *Anthology of Concretism*, ed. Eugene Wildman.
19   'Two Women Poets: One Old, One New', *New York
     Times Book Review* (11 November), pp. 42–4 (Review of

*Studies for an Actress* by Jean Garrigue and *The Plenitude We Cry For* by Sarah Appleton).

## 1974

20  *Once More Out of Darkness and Other Poems* (Poetry) (Berkeley: Berkeley Poets' Cooperative), 32 pp.
21  'Girls, Ladies and Women', *Parnassus* 3, no. 1 (Fall/ Winter), pp. 185–91 (Review of *False Trees* by Rochelle Ratner, *Moscow Mansions* by Barbara Guest, *Life Notes* and *No Hassles* by Anne Waldman, *A Desperate Thing* by Norma Farber, and *Cup of Cold Water* by Siv Cedering Fox).
22  'Won't and Will Take Yes For an Answer', *New York Times Book Review* (17 February), pp. 7–8 (Review of *Cruelty* by Ai, *Mink Coat* by Jill Hoffman, and *In the Temperate Zone* by Judith Kroll). 'Ai' excerpted and reprinted in *Contemporary Literary Criticism* 4 (1975), p. 16.

## 1975

23  'Ai', in *Contemporary Literary Criticism* 4, ed. Carolyn Riley (Detroit: Gale Research Co.), p. 16. Excerpted from 'Won't and Will Take Yes For an Answer', *New York Times Book Review* (17 February, 1974), pp. 7–8.
24  'Sex Discrimination in the Universities', *Women's Rights Law Reporter* 2 (Newark, NJ) (March), pp. 3–12. With Leigh Bienen and J. P. Ostriker. Reprinted in *Woman in a Man-made World* (1977), pp. 370–77.
25  Review of *William Blake* by D. G. Gillham, *Blake Newsletter* 32, vol. 8, no. 4 (Spring), pp. 136–7.

## 1976

26  'Paul Goodman', *Partisan Review* 43, no. 2 (Summer), pp. 286–95 (Essay on Goodman's poetry). Reprinted as

'Poet of Indecorum', in *Artist of the Actual: Essays on Paul Goodman* (1986), pp. 80–9.


## 1977

27  (Ed.), *William Blake: The Complete Poems* (New York: Penguin), 1071 pp., Notes, pp. 870–1057.
28  'The Nerves of a Midwife: Contemporary American Women's Poetry', *Parnassus* 6, no. 1 (Fall/Winter), pp. 69–87. Reprinted in *The Pushcart Prize IV: Best of the Small Presses* (1979), pp. 451–69. Also reprinted in *Claims for Poetry* (1982), pp. 309–27, and in *Poetics: Essays on the Art of Poetry* (1984), pp. 111–38.
29  'A Quiet Rape in A Quiet Town' (under the pseudonym Ruth Miller), *Village Voice* 21, no. 9 (28 February), pp. 19, 20, 22.
30  'Sex Discrimination in the Universities' (with Leigh Bienen and J. P. Ostriker), in *Woman in a Man-made World: A Socioeconomic Handbook* (2nd edn), ed. Nona Glazer and Helen Youngelson Waehrer (New York: Rand McNally), pp. 370–77. Reprinted from *Women's Rights Law Reporter* 2 (March 1975), pp. 3–12.
31  'Shapes of Poetry', *Partisan Review* 44, no. 4 (Fall), pp. 632–6 (Review of *Vision and Resonance: Two Senses of Poetic Form* by John Hollander). Reprinted in *Contemporary Literary Criticism* 14 (1980), pp. 262–3.


## 1978

32  'May Swenson and the Shapes of Speculation', *American Poetry Review* 7, no. 2 (March/April), pp. 35–8. Reprinted in *Shakespeare's Sisters* (1979), pp. 221–32. Also reprinted in *Contemporary Literary Criticism* 14 (1980), p. 518.
33  'Ideas of Order in Rochester', *Canto* 2, no. 1 (Spring), pp. 173–80 (Review of *Millions of Strange Shadows* by Anthony Hecht). Reprinted as '*Millions of Strange Shadows*: Anthony Hecht as Gentile and Jew' in *The Burdens of Formality: Essays on the Poetry of Anthony Hecht* (1989), pp. 97–105.

**1979**

34  *A Dream of Springtime: Poems 1970–78* (Poetry) (New York: Smith/Horizon Press), 61 pp.

35  'Her Cargo: Adrienne Rich and the Common Language', *American Poetry Review* 8, no. 4 (July/August), pp. 6–10. Excerpted in *Contemporary Literary Criticism* 36 (1986), pp. 372–4. Reprinted in *Writing Like a Woman* (1983), pp. 102–25.

36  'May Swenson and the Shapes of Speculation', in *Shakespeare's Sisters: Feminist Essays on Women Poets*, eds Sandra M. Gilbert and Susan Gubar (Bloomington, Ind.: Indiana University Press), pp. 221–32. Reprinted from *American Poetry Review* 7, no. 2 (March/April 1978), pp. 35–8. Also reprinted in *Contemporary Literary Criticism* 14 (1980), p. 518.

37  'The Nerves of a Midwife: Contemporary American Women's Poetry', in *The Pushcart Prize IV: Best of the Small Presses*, ed. Bill Henderson (Yonkers, NY: Pushcart Press), pp. 451–69. Reprinted from *Parnassus* 6, no. 1 (Fall/Winter 1977), pp. 69–87. Reprinted in *Claims for Poetry* (1982), pp. 309–27. Also reprinted in *Poetics: Essays on the Art of Poetry* (1984), pp. 111–38.

**1980**

38  *The Mother/Child Papers* (Poetry) (Los Angeles: Momentum Press), 62 pp. Reprinted, 1986 (Boston: Beacon Press).

39  'Body Language: Imagery of the Body in Women's Poetry', in *The State of the Language*, ed. Leonard Michaels and Christopher Ricks (Los Angeles and Berkeley: University of California Press), pp. 247–63. Revised version reprinted in chapter 3 of *Stealing the Language* (1986).

40  'May Swenson and the Shapes of Speculation', in *Contemporary Literary Criticism* 14, eds Dedria Bryfonski and Laurie Lanzen Harris (Detroit: Gale Research Co.), p. 518. Reprinted from *American Poetry Review* 7, no. 2

(March/April 1978), pp. 35–8. Also reprinted in *Shakespeare's Sisters: Feminist Essays on Women Poets* (1979), pp. 221–32.

41   'Drought and Flood', *Partisan Review* 47, no. 1 (Winter), pp. 153–61 (Review of *Sphere: The Form of a Motion* by A. R. Ammons, *Lady of the Beasts* by Robin Morgan, and *Ginkgo* by Felix Pollak).

42   'Shapes of Poetry', in *Contemporary Literary Criticism* 14, eds Dedria Bryfonski and Laurie Lanzen Harris (Detroit: Gale Research Co.), pp. 262–3. Reprinted from *Partisan Review* 44, no. 4 (Fall 1977), pp. 632–6 (Review of *Vision and Resonance: Two Senses of Poetic Form* by John Hollander).

43   Review of Four New Poets, *American Book Review* (Spring).

44   Review of *Wollstonecraft Anthology*, ed. Janet M. Todd, *Blake Quarterly* (Fall), pp. 129–31.


## 1981

45   'Fact as Style: the Americanization of Sylvia', *Contemporary Literary Criticism* 17, ed. Sharon R. Gunton, pp. 348–9. Reprinted from *Language and Style* 1, no. 3 (Summer 1968), pp. 201–12. Reprinted as 'The Americanization of Sylvia', in *Writing Like a Woman* (1983), pp. 42–58. Also reprinted in *Critical Essays on Sylvia Plath* (1984), pp. 97–109.

46   Review of *Blake 'and' Freud* by Diana Hume George, *Wordsworth Circle* 12, no. 3 (Summer), pp. 161–4.


## 1982

47   *A Woman Under the Surface* (Poetry) Series of Contemporary Poets (Princeton: Princeton University Press), 78 pp.

48   'Blake, Ginsberg, Madness and the Poet as Shaman', in *Blake and the Moderns*, eds Robert Berthoff and Annette Leavitt (Albany, NY: SUNY Press), pp. 111–31.

49  'Desire Gratified and Ungratified: Blake and Sexuality',
    *Blake: An Illustrated Quarterly* 16, no. 3 (Winter), pp.
    156–65.
50  'The Nerves of a Midwife: Contemporary American
    Women's Poetry', in *Claims for Poetry*, ed. Donald Hall
    (Ann Arbor, Mich.: University of Michigan Press), pp.
    309–27. Reprinted from *Parnassus* 6, no. 1 (Fall/Winter
    1977), pp. 69–87. Reprinted in *The Pushcart Prize IV: Best
    of the Small Presses* (1979), pp. 451–69. Also reprinted in
    *Poetics: Essays on the Art of Poetry* (1984), pp. 111–38.
51  'That Story: Anne Sexton and Her Transformations',
    *American Poetry Review* 11, no. 4 (July/August), pp. 11–
    16. Reprinted as 'That Story: The Changes of Anne
    Sexton', in *Writing Like a Woman* (1983), pp. 59–85.
    Also excerpted in *Twentieth-Century American Literature*,
    volume 6 of *The Chelsea House Library of Literary Criticism*
    (1987), pp. 3596–601. Also reprinted in *Sexton: Selected
    Criticism* (1988), pp. 251–73.
52  'The Thieves of Language: Women Poets and Revisionist
    Mythmaking', *Signs* 8, no. 1 (Autumn), pp. 68–90. Re-
    printed in *The New Feminist Criticism* (1985), pp. 314–
    38. Also reprinted in *Coming to Light* (1985), pp. 10–36.
    Revised version also reprinted in chapter 6 of *Stealing the
    Language* (1986).
53  'Memory and Attachment', *New York Times Book Review*
    (8 August), pp. 10, 22 (Review of *Our Ground Time Here
    Will Be Brief* and *Why Can't We Live Together Like Civil-
    ized Human Beings* by Maxine Kumin). Reprinted in *Con-
    temporary Literary Criticism* 28 (1984), pp. 224–5.
54  Review of *Admit Impediment* by Marie Ponsot, *13th Moon*
    6, nos 1/2, pp. 145–7.
55  Review of *The Madwoman in the Attic* by Sandra M.
    Gilbert and Susan Gubar and *Madness in Literature* by
    Lillian Feder, *American Book Review* 4, no. 3
    (March/April), p. 7.

## 1983

56  *Writing Like a Woman*, Poets on Poetry Series (Ann
    Arbor, Mich.: University of Michigan Press), 147 pp.

Essays on H.D., Sylvia Plath, Anne Sexton, May Swenson, Adrienne Rich, and two personal essays.

57 'In Mind: The Divided Self and Women's Poetry', *The Midwest Quarterly* 24, no. 4 (Summer), pp. 351–6. Revised version reprinted in chapter 2 of *Stealing the Language* (1986). Also reprinted in *Poetics: Essays on the Art of Poetry* (1984), pp. 111–38.

58 'The Poet as Heroine: Learning to Read H.D.', *American Poetry Review* 12, no. 2 (March/April), pp. 29–38.

59 Review of *The Continuing City: William Blake's 'Jerusalem'* by Morton Paley, *The Eighteenth Century: A Current Bibliography*, n.s. 9 (for 1983), ed. Jim Springer Borck (New York: AMS Press, 1988), pp. 532–3.

60 Review of *Natural Birth* by Toi Dericotte, *13th Moon* 7, nos 1/2, pp. 183–5.

## 1984

61 'The Americanization of Sylvia', in *Critical Essays on Sylvia Plath*, ed. Linda Wagner (Boston: G. K. Hall), pp. 97–109. Reprinted from *Language and Style* 1, no. 3 (Summer 1968), pp. 201–12. Also reprinted in *Writing Like a Woman* (1983), pp. 42–58, and in *Contemporary Literary Criticism* 17 (1981), pp. 348–9.

62 'In Mind: The Divided Self and Women's Poetry', in *Poetics: Essays on the Art of Poetry* (An Anthology from *Tendril* magazine), compiled by Paul Mariani and George Murphy, pp. 111–38. Reprinted from *The Midwest Quarterly* 24, no. 4 (Summer 1983), pp. 351–6. Revised version reprinted in chapter 2 of *Stealing the Language* (1986).

63 'Memory and Attachment', in *Contemporary Literary Criticism* 28, ed. Jean C. Stine (Detroit: Gale Research Co.), pp. 224–5. Reprinted from *New York Times Book Review* (8 August 1982), pp. 10, 22 (Review of *Our Ground Time Here Will Be Brief* and *Why Can't We Live Together Like Civilized Human Beings* by Maxine Kumin).

64 'The Nerves of a Midwife: Contemporary American Women's Poetry', in *Poetics: Essays on the Art of Poetry*

(An Anthology from *Tendril* magazine), compiled by Paul Mariani and George Murphy, pp. 111–38. Reprinted from *Parnassus* 6, no. 1 (Fall/Winter 1977), pp. 69–87. Also reprinted in *The Pushcart Prize IV: Best of the Small Presses* (1979), pp. 451–69. Also reprinted in *Claims for Poetry* (1982), pp. 309–27.

65 ' "What Are Patterns For?", Anger and Polarization in Women's Poetry', *Feminist Studies* 10, no. 3 (Fall), pp. 485–503. Revised version reprinted in chapter 4 of *Stealing the Language* (1986). Excerpted in *Critical Essays on Anne Sexton* (1989), pp. 186–93.

66 Review of *Infernal Poetic Structures in Blake's 'Lambeth Prophecies'* by John Howard, *The Eighteenth Century: A Current Bibliography*, n. s. 10 (for 1984), ed. Jim Springer Borck (New York: AMS Press, 1989), pp. 562–3.

67 Review of *Sex and Sensibility: Ideal and Erotic Love from Milton to Mozart* by Jean H. Hagstrum, *Blake: An Illustrated Quarterly* 18 (Summer), pp. 52–3.


### 1985

68 'A Different Yes: The Imperative of Intimacy', *Poetry Flash: The Bay Area's Poetry Calendar and Review* 149 (August), pp. 1, 3.

69 'Anti-Critic', in *Contemporary Literary Criticism* 31, eds Jean C. Stine and Daniel G. Marowski, pp. 405–6. Reprinted from *Commentary* 41, no. 5 (June 1966), pp. 83–4 (Review of *Against Interpretation* by Susan Sontag).

70 'The Thieves of Language: Women Poets and Revisionist Mythmaking', in *The New Feminist Criticism*, ed. Elaine Showalter (New York: Pantheon Books), pp. 314–38. Also published in *Coming to Light: American Women Poets in the Twentieth Century*, eds Diane Wood Middlebrook and Marilyn Yalom (Ann Arbor, Mich.: University of Michigan Press), pp. 10–36. Reprinted from *Signs* 8, no. 1 (Autumn 1982), pp. 66–90.

71 'Being Nobody Together: Duplicity, Identity, and Women's Poetry', *Parnassus* 12/13, nos 2/1 (Spring/Summer, Fall/Winter), pp. 201–22 (women's poetry issue).

Revised version reprinted in chapter 2 of *Stealing the Language* (1986).

72  'Reply to Hagstrum', *Blake: an Illustrated Quarterly* 18, no. 4 (Spring), p. 238.

73  ' "What Do Women (Poets) Want?": Marianne Moore and H.D. as Poetic Ancestresses', *Poesis* 6, no. 1 (Spring; Moore/H.D. issue), pp. 1–9 (given as keynote address at the Bryn Mawr College English Department Symposium on H.D. and Marianne Moore in April 1985). Excerpted in *Poetry Project: the Newsletter of the Poetry Project at St Mark's Church-in-the-Bowery* 114 (May). Revised version in *Contemporary Literature* 27, no. 4 (Winter 1986–7), pp. 475–92.

74  'Innocence of Heart and Violence of Feeling', *New York Times Book Review* (3 March), pp. 1, 30 (Review of *Louise Bogan, A Portrait* by Elizabeth Frank). Reprinted in *Contemporary Literary Criticism* 39 (1986), pp. 387–8.


## 1986


75  *The Imaginary Lover* (Poetry) Pitt Poetry Series (Pittsburgh: University of Pittsburgh Press), 110 pp.

76  *Stealing the Language: The Emergence of Women's Poetry in America* (Boston: Beacon Press), xvii, 315 pp.

77  'American Poetry, Now Shaped by Women', *New York Times Book Review* (9 March), pp. 1, 28, 30. Translated in *International Literature* (1987).

78  'Her Cargo: Adrienne Rich and the Common Language', in *Contemporary Literary Criticism* 36, ed. Daniel G. Marowski (Detroit: Gale Research Co.), pp. 372–4. Excerpted from *American Poetry Review* 8, no. 4 (July/August 1979), pp. 6–10. Reprinted in *Writing Like a Woman* (1983), pp. 102–25.

79  'Poet of Indecorum', in *Artist of the Actual: Essays on Paul Goodman*, ed. Peter Parisi (Metuchen, NJ and London: Scarecrow Press), pp. 80–9. Reprinted from 'Paul Goodman', *Partisan Review* 43, no. 2 (Summer 1976), pp. 286–95.

80  ' "What Do Women (Poets) Want?": Marianne Moore and H. D. as Poetic Ancestresses', in *Contemporary Lit-*

*erature* 27, no. 4 (Winter), pp. 475–92. Revised from original publication in *Poesis* 6, no. 1 (Spring 1985), pp. 1–9. Excerpted in *Poetry Project: The Newsletter of the Poetry Project at St Mark's Church-in-the-Bowery* 114 (May 1985).

81 'Innocence of Heart and Violence of Feeling', in *Contemporary Literary Criticism* 39, ed. Sharon K. Hall (Detroit: Gale Research Co.), pp. 387–8. Reprinted from *New York Times Book Review* (3 March 1985), pp. 1, 30 (Review of *Louise Bogan, A Portrait* by Elizabeth Frank).

82 'Job: Or the Imagination of Justice', *Iowa Review* 10, no. 3 (Fall), pp. 87–92.

83 'Natural Facts', *The Nation* 243, no. 5 (23 August), pp. 148–50 (Review of *The Happy Man* by Donald Hall and *Dream Work* by Mary Oliver).


### 1987

84 'American Poetry, Now Shaped by Women', *International Literature*, trans. Lili Wang. Reprinted from *New York Times Book Review* (9 March 1986), pp. 1, 28, 30.

85 'Dancing at the Devil's Party: Some Notes on Politics and Poetry', *Critical Inquiry* 13, no. 3 (Spring), pp. 579–96. Reprinted in *Politics and Poetic Value*, ed. Robert von Hallberg (Chicago and London: University of Chicago Press), pp. 207–24. Also reprinted in *Conversant Essays: Contemporary Poets on Poetry* (1990), pp. 399–413.

86 'The Lyric: The Poetry', in *The New History of Literature: English Poetry and Prose 1540–1674* (New York: Peter Bedrick Books), pp. 91–106. Originally published as 'The Lyric', in *English Poetry and Prose 1540–1674*, volume 2 in the *History of Literature in the English Language* (1970), pp. 119–36.

87 'That Story: Anne Sexton and Her Transformations', in *Twentieth-Century American Literature*, volume 6 of *The Chelsea House Library of Literary Criticism*, ed. Harold Bloom (New York: Chelsea House Publishers), pp. 3596–601. Excerpted from *American Poetry Review* 11, no. 4 (July/August 1982), pp. 11–16. Also reprinted in *Sexton: Selected Criticism* (1988), pp. 251–73.

88  'The Tune of Crisis', *Poetry* 149, no. 1 (January), pp. 231–7 (Review of *Your Native Land, Your Life* by Adrienne Rich, *The Gold Cell* by Sharon Olds, *Sin* by Ai, and *A Fish to Feed All Hunger* by Sandra Alcossar).

89  Review of *Oedipus Anne: The Poetry of Anne Sexton* by Diana George, *New England Quarterly* (Fall), pp. 652–6.

## 1988

90  'Anne Sexton and the Seduction of the Audience', in *Sexton: Selected Criticism*, ed. Diana Hume George (Urbana, Ill.: University of Illinois Press), pp. 3–18. Reprinted in *Seduction and Theory* (1989), pp. 154–69.

91  'That Story: Anne Sexton and Her Transformations', in *Sexton: Selected Criticism*, ed. Diana Hume George (Urbana, Ill.: University of Illinois Press), pp. 251–73. Reprinted from *American Poetry Review* 11, no. 4 (July/August 1982), pp. 11–16. Also reprinted in *Twentieth-Century American Literature*, volume 6 of *The Chelsea House Library of Literary Criticism* (1987), pp. 3596–601.

92  'The Garden', *Michigan Quarterly Review* 27, no. 3 (Summer), pp. 388–94.

93  'Intensive Care', *Santa Monica Review*, 1, no. 1 (Fall), pp. 31–6.

94  'The Old Testament and Feminist Imagination', *Associated Writing Programs Newsletter* 21 (September), p. 10.

95  'Love and Power in Women's Poetry', *P.E.N. Newsletter* 65 (June) (women's issue), pp. 11–12.

96  'No Rule of Procedure: The Open Poetics of H. D.', *Agenda* 25, nos 3/4 (Autumn/Winter), pp. 145–54 (special issue on H. D.). Reprinted in *Signets: Reading H. D.* (1990), pp. 336–51. Excerpted in *How(ever)* 5, no. 4 (Fall 1989), pp. 20–1.

## 1989

97  *Green Age* (Poetry) Pitt Poetry Series (Pittsburgh: University of Pittsburgh Press), 75 pp.

98 'Anne Sexton and the Seduction of the Audience', in Seduction and Theory, ed. Dianne Hunter (Urbana, Ill.: University of Illinois Press, 1989), pp. 154–69. Reprinted from Sexton: Selected Criticism (1988), pp. 3–18.

99 'Comment on Claire Kahane: Questioning the Maternal Voice', Genders 4 (March), pp. 130–3.

100 'Entering the Tents', Feminist Studies 15, no. 3 (Fall), pp. 541–7. Excerpted from The Nakedness of the Fathers, forthcoming.

101 'The Story of Joshua', Lilith 14, no. 4 (Fall), p. 20.

102 'The Story of Noah', Lilith 14, no. 4 (Fall), pp. 19–20.

103 'Time Passes', Lilith 14, no. 4 (Fall), p. 18.

104 'Millions of Strange Shadows: Anthony Hecht as Gentile and Jew', in The Burdens of Formality: Essays on the Poetry of Anthony Hecht, ed. Sydney Lea (Athens, Ga.: University of Georgia Press), pp. 97–105. Reprinted from 'Ideas of Order in Rochester', Canto 2, no. 1 (Spring 1978), pp. 173–80.

105 'No Rule of Procedure: H. D. and Open Poetics', excerpted in How(ever) 5, no. 4 (Fall) ('Lyric Proposals' issue), pp. 20–1. Reprinted from Agenda 25, nos 3/4 (Autumn/Winter 1988), pp. 145–54. Reprinted in Signets: Reading H. D. (1990), pp. 336–51.

106 'The Poetic Process: Three Poets on Poetry', Poetry Society of America Newsletter 31 (Fall), pp. 1, 4–8 (three-way interview with Carolyn Forche and Sharon Olds).

107 'Readings: An Interview with Alicia Ostriker', Poets & Writers 17, no. 6 (November/December), pp. 16–26 (Interviewed by Katharyn Machan Aal).

108 'Response to Bonnie Costello', Contemporary Literature 30, no. 3 (Fall), pp. 462–4. Reply to review of Stealing the Language (1986) in Contemporary Literature 29, no. 2 (Summer 1988), pp. 305–10.

109 ' "What Are Patterns For?", Anger and Polarization in Women's Poetry', in Critical Essays on Anne Sexton, ed. Linda Wagner-Martin (Boston: G. K. Hall), pp. 186–93. Excerpted from Feminist Studies 10, no. 3 (Fall 1984), pp. 485–503. Also reprinted in chapter 4 of Stealing the Language (1986).

## 1990

110    'Dancing at the Devil's Party: Some Notes on Politics
       and Poetry', in *Conversant Essays: Contemporary Poets on
       Poetry*, ed. James McCorkle (Detroit: Wayne State
       University Press), pp. 399–413. Reprinted from *Critical
       Inquiry* 13, no. 3 (Spring 1987), pp. 579–96. Also re-
       printed in *Politics and Poetic Value* (1987), pp. 207–24.

111    'Marianne Moore, the Maternal Hero, and American
       Women's Poetry', in *Marianne Moore: The Art of a Mod-
       ernist*, ed. Joseph Parisi (Ann Arbor, Mich.: University
       Microfilms International Research Press), pp. 49–66.

112    'The Passion of Sarah and the Opinion of Hagar',
       *Tikkun* (September), pp. 52–3.

113    'No Rule of Procedure: H. D. and Open Poetics', in
       *Signets: Reading H. D.*, eds Susan Stanford Friedman
       and Rachel Blau DuPlessis (Madison, Wis.: Univer-
       sity of Wisconsin Press), pp. 336–51. Reprinted from
       *Agenda* 25, nos 3/4 (Autumn/Winter 1988), pp. 145–
       54. Excerpted in *How(ever)* 5, no. 4 (Fall 1989), pp.
       20–1.

114    'The Road of Excess: My William Blake', in *The Ro-
       mantics and Us: Essays on Romantic and Modern Culture*,
       ed. Gene W. Ruoff (New Brunswick, NJ: Rutgers
       University Press), pp. 67–88.

115    'Cain and Abel: A Question of Ethics', *Ontario Review*
       32 (Spring/Summer), pp. 83–4.

116    'The Cave', *Ontario Review* 32 (Spring/Summer), pp.
       85–8.

117    'The Wisdom of Solomon', *Kenyon Review* 12, no. 2
       (Spring), pp. 149–55.

118    'From a New Past to a New Future', *Women's Review
       of Books* 7, no. 12 (September), p. 12 (Review of *Stand-
       ing Again at Sinai: Judaism from a Feminist Perspective* by
       Judith Plaskow).

119    Review of *Sarah's Daughters Sing: A Sampler of Poems by
       Jewish Women* by Henny Wenkart, *Lilith* 15, no. 3
       (Summer), p. 6.

**1991/1992**

120  'My Name is Laughter: Irving Feldman and the Re-
     playing of the *Akedah*', in *The Poetry of Irving Feldman:
     Nine Essays*, ed. Harold Schweizer (Lewisburg, Pa.:
     Bucknell University Press, 1991), pp. 101–25.

121  'Cry Wolf', in *The Critical Response to Tom Wolfe*, ed.
     Doug Shoumette (Westport, Conn.: Greenwood Press,
     1992), pp. 51–3 (Review of *Radical Chic and Mau-
     Mauing the Flak Catchers* by Tom Wolfe). Reprinted
     from *Partisan Review* 38, no. 3 (Summer 1971), pp.
     355–8.

122  '1985', in *Taking Note: From Poets' Notebooks, Seneca
     Review* 21, no. 2 (1991).

123  'Esther, or the World Turned Upside Down', *Kenyon
     Review* 13, no. 3 (Summer, 1991), pp. 18–21.

124  'Indecent Exposure?', *Women's Review of Books* 9, no. 2
     (November 1991), pp. 1, 3–4 (Review of *Anne Sexton:
     A Biography* by Diane Middlebrook).

125  'Loving Walt Whitman and the Problem of America',
     in *The Continuing Presence of Walt Whitman: the Life
     After the Life*, ed. Robert K. Martin (Iowa City: Univer-
     sity of Iowa Press, 1992), pp. 217–31.

126  'A Word Made Flesh: the Bible and Revisionist
     Women's Poetry', *Religion and Literature* 23, no. 3 (Fall
     1991), pp. 9–26.

127  'Some Notes of A on *The Book of J*', *Iowa Review* 21,
     no. 3 (Fall 1991), pp. 11–18 (A forum on *The Book of
     J*).

128  'Liberated Theology', *Tikkun* (March/April 1991), pp.
     43–5 (Review of *The Book of J* by David Rosenberg and
     Harold Bloom).

129  'The Interpretation of Dreams', Kenyon Review 13, no. 3
     (Summer), pp. 17–22.

# Index